ashley

D1142230

First published in Great Britain by HarperCollins*Entertainment* 2004
HarperCollins*Entertainment* is an imprint of HarperCollins*Publishers* Ltd, 77-85 Fulham Palace Road, Hammersmith, London W6 8JB

Text © HarperCollins*Publishers* 2004

Now You See Him, Now You Don't
First published in the USA by HarperEntertainment 2002
First published in Great Britain by HarperCollins*Entertainment* 2003
TWO OF A KIND characters, names and all related indicia are trademarks of Warner Bros. TM & ©2000.

The HarperCollins children's website address is
www.harpercollinschildrensbooks.co.uk

The Mary-Kate and Ashley website address is
www.mary-kateandashley.com

1 3 5 7 9 10 8 6 4 2

ISBN 0 00 718136 1

Printed and bound in Spain

Conditions of sale
This book is sold subject to the condition that it shall not, by way of trade or otherwise, be lent, re-sold, hired out otherwise circulated without the publisher's written consent in any form of binding or cover other than that in which is is published and without a similar condition, including this condition, being imposed on the subsequent purchaser.

Pictures ™ and © 2004 Dualstar Entertainment Group, LLC

Louise
Morgan

The Ultimate Guide to
Mary-Kate and Ashley

www.mary-kateandashley.com

DUALSTAR
PUBLICATIONS

HarperCollins*Entertainment*

Contents

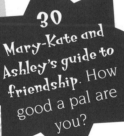

Hi! Welcome to The Ultimate Guide to Mary-Kate and Ashley! This is where we get to share with you all our secrets, and pass on all the hints and tips we've picked up on how to look and feel great. There are quizzes, puzzles and games and, just for you, one story from our *Two of a Kind* book series.

We hope you absolutely love it!

With love from

Mary-Kate Ashley

Catch up with
Mary-Kate and Ashley

Here's the inside scoop on what Mary-Kate and Ashley have been up to over the past few years…

1986
Mary-Kate and Ashley were born on 13 June 1986. Here they are age six months.

1987
In February 1987, age seven months, Mary-Kate and Ashley went to their first audition, and got the part of baby Michelle Tanner in a sitcom called *Full House*. Because they were so young they shared the role.

1992
That was the year Mary-Kate and Ashley shot their first television movie, *To Grandmother's House We Go*. They filmed it during summer break, and when it was shown on TV it was one of the most-watched movies of the season.

**FunFact
1992**
This was the year that Mary-Kate rode her first horse!

1993
This was a really busy year for Mary-Kate and Ashley. In April they released their first music video, *Our First Video*, and then in November they played private investigators called 'The Trenchcoat Twins' for a new video and book series, *The Adventures of Mary-Kate and Ashley*.

FunFact
1996
Mary-Kate and Ashley both lost their front teeth while on location in Florida!

1995

This was the year that Mary-Kate and Ashley made their first feature film, *It Takes Two*, in Toronto. In it, the girls play identical 'strangers', one rich and one poor. When they discover each other, they come up with a scheme to make their guardians fall in love. The movie was a huge success.

1996

This was a really exciting year for Mary-Kate and Ashley because the entire family went on a Hawaiin surf-and-sun holiday while they made some videos there!

1998

This year Mary-Kate and Ashley starred in their television series, *Two of a Kind*.

1999

Mary-Kate and Ashley joined their 11th grade cheerleading squad and had their first on-screen kisses, when they filmed *Passport to Paris*!

2000

Mary-Kate and Ashley visited the UK while they filmed *Winning London*. Here they are sight-seeing!

FunFact
2001
The girls had a new series on TV called *So Little Time*.

2002

Mary-Kate and Ashley went to Italy to film the movie *When in Rome*. But they still made time to do lots of studying to get ready for college and their SATs. They also passed their driving tests!

2003

Mary-Kate and Ashley produced and starred in their feature film *New York Minute*.

2004

Mary-Kate and Ashley were accepted to and started college in New York.

Mary-Kate and Ashley's
groovy guide to fashion and style

Mary-Kate and Ashley just *loooove* fashion, so much so that they've even helped design their own fashion range – how cool is that?

What's your fashion style? Find out with this quick quiz.

STYLE SECRET
Cool accessories can really update an outfit!

You're off on a school geography trip and you'll be traipsing through muddy fields all day. You make sure you've got:

A a spare set of false nails in case you break one of your own

B that toasty lime and orange striped sweater your Gran made for you – the one that reaches down to your knees

C a funky backpack crammed with loads of useful stuff – snacks, a torch, water…

Fab news – for your birthday, your mum and dad are letting you take your ten best friends anywhere you like! You choose:

A hiring a DJ and having your own disco – glitter, music and glitz galore!

B an afternoon tea party with cake

C everyone sees a movie, then go on for a pizza afterwards

STYLE SECRET
You can buy fashion, but you can't buy style!

FASHION TIP
Smiles never go out of fashion!

Your dream night out would be

 A going to a movie premiere and rubbing shoulders with the stars

 B you'd rather stay in and catch up on your favourite soaps.

 C a party with all your friends so you can dress up a bit, gossip, groove to the music and grab some crisps and dips

FASHION TIP
Jeans +
T-Shirt
= perfect!

As a treat for doing well at school, your parents are buying you an outfit of your choice. You go for

A anything with sequins and sparkle – and you can't wait to wear it to the next party

B you have enough clothes, but you could use some more socks and a couple of vests

C some cool cropped jeans and a cute top to wear with your mates during the weekend

Mostly A's
PARTY QUEEN!
You know all about dressing to impress, but don't forget style is for everyday, not just the big occasions. Make sure you have a few toned-down outfits for when you don't want to do the full fashion thing.

Mostly B's
NO-STRESS DRESSER!
You have more important things on your mind than fashion, but hey, that's cool – have the confidence to stick with your own style and ignore the fashionistas!

Mostly C's
ALL RIGHT ON THE NIGHT!
When it comes to fashion, it's not the be all and end all, but you usually manage to look pretty good. You dress for the occasion and don't let yourself become a fashion victim.
Well done!

STYLE
SECRET

Style is all about
being confident with
who you are.

The ultimate A-Z of
Mary-Kate and Ashley

A Mary-Kate and Ashley often sign **autographs** for their fans. A film producer once tried to disguise Mary-Kate with sunglasses and a big hat, to smuggle her past the fans and on to the film set, but the fans recognised her anyway!

B For their sixteenth **birthdays**, Mary-Kate and Ashley each got a birthday cake decorated to look like a driver's licence, complete with their pictures on it!

C When Mary-Kate and Ashley filmed *The Adventures of Mary-Kate and Ashley Hotel Who-Done-It*, there was a scene where the girls had to eat loads of **chocolate**. Mary-Kate says "I was in total heaven!"

D Ashley loves ballet, and she had a blast making the video *Ballet Party* with the New York City Ballet. "I got to live out one of my big **dreams**!" she says.

E When they were filming *You're Invited to Mary-Kate and Ashley's Birthday Party*, the sisters had to ride a roller coaster **eight** times in a row – they got so dizzy they could hardly stand up!

F What will Mary-Kate and Ashley do in the **future**? So far, they know they are going to college and may get involved in film directing, but anything is possible.

G Mary-Kate admits "I do have one big weakness. **Gum.** I'll stuff five pieces in my mouth if no one is looking!" Oh well, no one's perfect!

H Meanwhile, we hear that Ashley, too, has a major weakness – **handbags**!

I As the girls get older, their movies reflect the changes they're going through. That's why **independence** was such a strong theme in their film *Getting There*. It's about a road trip, and in real life the girls were just learning to drive.

J Don't you think Mary-Kate and Ashley have the coolest **jobs** in the whole world? They get to travel, meet new people and see new places all the time!

K Mary-Kate and Ashley came to London to film *Winning London*, and visited Westminster Abbey where most of England's **kings** and queens have been crowned. Ashley says "It was an amazing feeling being in such an historic church."

L Mary-Kate remembers a special occasion when they and their friends went to a restaurant in a **limousine.** Ashley says "I prefer driving myself than riding in a limo."

M When it comes to **make-up**, both girls like the fresh-faced look with a hint of lip gloss, but they love to glam up if they're going somewhere special.

N Believe it or not, Mary-Kate and Ashley still get **nervous** in front of an audience – they get butter-flies just like you do when you have to stand up and give a speech at school.

O Mary-Kate and Ashley do have occasional differences, like when they both want to wear the same **outfit** – but they talk it over and usually decide to take turns!

P While filming *To Grandmother's House We Go*, Mary-Kate scratched her eye. It was so red that, for one scene where they appeared together, Ashley had to dress as Mary-Kate and play both **parts**. Now that really is double trouble!

Q So, do Mary-Kate and Ashley have any plans to **quit** what they're doing? "No. We love what we're doing," Ashley says.

R When she was little, Mary-Kate made a plan to **run** away to Canada so she could visit her favourite horse – luckily her dad caught her while she was packing!

S When they were filming *Passport to Paris*, the girls went to a restaurant and ordered – **snails**! These are a delicacy in France. Ashley thought they were 'tres bon' (very good), but Mary-Kate's verdict was 'Yuk!'

T People often ask the girls if it's fun being a **twin**. Their answer? A great big 'Yes!'

U Mary-Kate and Ashley are **unique** in being the first teens ever to produce and star in their own television series – *So Little Time*!

V When filming *Our Lips Are Sealed* in Australia, the girls found themselves acting with a kangaroo called **Vince**. Apparently he was so cute, they wanted to take him home!

W In their movie *The Challenge* Mary-Kate had to eat a worm! It was only a brown Gummi **Worm**, but she still had to put her hand into a plate of real ones – how brave is that?

X **XXX** Filming *Passport to Paris*, Mary-Kate and Ashley had their first on-screen kiss in front of 50 people. No pressure there, then!

Y Mary-Kate and Ashley both love **yoga**. Try it – it's a great way to stay fit!

Z **Zzz**… When it comes to sleeping, Ashley likes to have a long lie in, while Mary-Kate likes to rise and shine early – even twins have their differences!

Now You See Him, Now You Don't

by Megan Stine

from the *Two of a Kind* book series created by
Robert Griffard & Howard Adler

CHAPTER ONE

"I'm in heaven," Mary-Kate Burke announced as she rushed through the doors of the White Oak cafeteria. "I've just had the most awesome afternoon of my entire life!"

Mary-Kate's sister Ashley glanced up from the powdered doughnut she was eating. She and a group of their friends were just finishing lunch.
"Where have you been?" Ashley asked.

"And what's his name?" Samantha Kramer joked. "There must be a guy involved if your day was that good."

What's his name? Mary-Kate's eyes twinkled. "Well," she said, "actually his name is Sugar."

Ashley sputtered powder in Mary-Kate's direction. "You spent the afternoon with a guy named Sugar?"

"Say it, don't spray it," Mary-Kate complained. "And Sugar is not a guy. He's a horse."

"A horse?" Ashley asked.

"The best horse ever," Mary-Kate declared. "I rode him all afternoon, and he was perfect!"

"I didn't know we had horseback riding at White Oak," Samantha said.

White Oak Academy was the all-girls boarding school they attended in New Hampshire.

"We don't," Mary-Kate explained as she took off her parka and squeezed next to Ashley on the bench.

"And I didn't know you rode," Phoebe Cahill said. Phoebe was Ashley's roommate. The girls were twelve years old and in the seventh grade.

"I started taking riding lessons back in Chicago when I was six," Mary-Kate said.

"She used to compete in show jumping," Ashley added. "Her room back home is filled with riding ribbons and trophies."

"I wish we did have riding here," Mary-Kate sighed. "I've missed it so much. My friend Charlotte heard me talking about it in gym the other day. So she introduced me to her friend Sean. His family owns the Starbright Stables – right down the road. He said I could come over any time I want to help him exercise the horses."

"It's funny that we're talking about horses," Phoebe said. "I just bought the greatest riding outfit. Vintage 1940s."

Mary-Kate rolled her eyes. Phoebe Cahill loved anything vintage. With her antique blue glasses, Phoebe herself looked as if she were living in the past. In fact, the only thing new in her room was her toothbrush!

"Sean wasn't there today," Mary-Kate went on. "So J.D. – he's one of the other stable boys – let me ride Sugar. Honestly, Ashley, he is the sweetest and smartest horse. Even you could ride him with no trouble!"

Ashley laughed. "I don't think so."

"What's the matter, Ashley?" Samantha asked. "Don't you like horses?"

"Sure, I like horses," Ashley said. "They just don't seem to like me."

"That's because you never learned to ride the right way," Mary-Kate said. "But you'd love Sugar, Ashley. He's the smartest horse I've ever ridden. And I've ridden a lot of horses." She smiled, remembering how well Sugar had responded to every command. "He's perfect." She sighed.

"Who's perfect?" a boy's voice behind Mary-Kate asked.

Mary-Kate whirled around. Ross Lambert and three of his friends were standing near the notice board behind her.

Ross was Ashley's boyfriend and a student at Harrington Academy, the all-boys school down the road.

Ashley jumped to her feet and gave Ross a big smile. "She's talking about a horse," she explained.

"What are you guys doing here?" Mary-Kate asked the boys.

"We came to put up these posters," Ross said. He reached into the bag he had slung over his shoulder. "The annual magic show is coming up." He pulled out a glossy poster showing a magician's top hat and magic wand.

"I heard something about that," Mary-Kate said. "It's for charity, right?"

Ross nodded. "It's a pretty big deal. People come from all the towns around here to see the show."

Elliot Weber, one of the guys with Ross, added, "Each magic act is performed by a team – a Harrington guy and a White Oak girl. It's been a tradition."

Ross turned round to tack the poster to the notice board. "We've got to hurry up and choose partners," he said. "The show is only a few weeks away." He smoothed the poster and turned back to face Ashley. "I already know who I want for a partner." He leaned close to Ashley and waggled his brown eyebrows, grinning. "Got any good tricks up your sleeve?"

"Me?" Ashley's face lit up. "Not yet, but I can find one if I have to."

"That's okay," Ross said. "I know a great trick we can do together. So we're a team?"

Ashley shook his hand. "We're a team."

"I want to be in the magic show, too," Mary-Kate said. "I already know one magic trick!" She grabbed the rest of Ashley's doughnut. "Now you see it—" She popped the doughnut in her mouth. "Now you don't!"

Everyone laughed. Mary-Kate looked at the three boys who had come with Ross. Would one of them be a good magic partner? she wondered.

There was Elliot Weber,

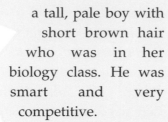

a tall, pale boy with short brown hair who was in her biology class. He was smart and very competitive.

He might be a good partner, Mary-Kate thought. Knowing Elliot, he'd want to make sure his trick was the best in the show.

Then there was Max Dorfman. He was short, with dark curly hair. He was shy and Mary-Kate didn't know him very well. The third boy was Marty Silver, who was always tripping over his own feet.

"I need a partner," Max said softly. "I'm going to pull a rabbit out of a hat."

Phoebe leaped to her feet. "I'll work with you! I love rabbits."

"Great," Max said. He gave a shy shrug and looked away.

"What kind of an act should we do?" Ashley asked Ross.

Ross shot her a smile. "I'm going to cut you in half," he said.

Ashley's jaw dropped. "You're kidding, right?"

"No, I'm serious," Ross said. "My uncle used to do magic tricks and he told me how the trick works."

Ross lowered his voice. Ashley and Mary-Kate leaned in so that they could hear. "He's got this special box," he whispered. "You have to cram yourself into a weird position so I can saw you in half without, you know, a lot of screaming and stuff."

"Very funny," Ashley said. "But seriously. Is it safe?"

"Totally," Ross said. "We're going to be the stars of the show!" he announced loudly.

"In your dreams!" Elliot shouted.

"What does that mean?" Ross asked.

"It means my trick is going to be way better than yours," Elliot bragged. "Just wait and see."

"What is your trick?" Ross demanded.

"Like I said, wait and see," Elliot said.

Mary-Kate tapped Elliot on the shoulder. "Can I be your partner?"

He pulled her aside. "That depends," he whispered. "Got any good ideas?"

"You mean you don't have a trick?" Mary-Kate's eyebrows shot up.

"Shhh! Not so loud!" Elliot said. "I know a lot of good tricks, but I need a really great one."

Mary-Kate racked her brain, trying to remember magic tricks she'd seen. "How about pulling a coin from behind my ear?"

Elliot rolled his eyes. "Try again," he said.

"Putting me in a box and making me disappear?" she suggested.

"Bor-ing," Elliot said. "I need to do something special. Something really different."

Mary-Kate thought for a minute. *What can we do that no one else can?* she wondered.

"I've got it!" Mary-Kate cried. "Elliot, what if I said I could teach a horse to do magic tricks?" She told Elliot all about Sugar.

Elliot smiled and stuck out his hand for Mary-Kate to shake. "I'd say welcome to the team!"

CHAPTER TWO

"Aren't you coming?" Ashley stood in the doorway to Mary-Kate's dorm room in Porter House the next afternoon. "The magic show rehearsal started ten minutes ago. We're late!"

Mary-Kate glanced up from the book she was reading. "Go ahead without me," she told Ashley. "Elliot and I aren't ready to rehearse yet. We've got a few details to work out first."

"Whatever you say," Ashley said. She glanced around her sister's room, staring at the softball trophies and posters of Derek Jeter and Sammy Sosa. Mary-Kate and her roommate, Campbell Smith, had totally different tastes than she and Phoebe did. Ashley's room was decorated with posters of poets and piles of soft throw pillows.

"Tell me all about it when you get back," Mary-Kate said.

"You got it," Ashley promised. "See you later."

Ashley hurried down the steps of Porter House and dashed outside. A cold gust of wind whipped her long blonde hair into her face. She ran across the snow-covered lawn to the shuttle bus stop just as the bus pulled up.

A few minutes later, it dropped her off at an old ivy-covered building that was Harrington's gymnasium and auditorium.

A sign on the door said: MAGIC SHOW REHEARSAL TODAY – NO ADMITTANCE.

Ashley tried the door. It was locked. *How am I supposed to rehearse if I can't get in?* she wondered.

She knocked as hard as she could. Finally the door opened a crack, and a boy's head peeked out.

"Jeremy?" Ashley said. Her cousin Jeremy was a student at Harrington. "Why is the door locked? Let me in!"

"No can do," Jeremy said. "The magicians are rehearsing. It's all top secret. No one's allowed in."

Ashley rolled her eyes. Her cousin Jeremy was the family jokester. He could also be the family pain.

"I'm supposed to be in there right now," Ashley insisted. "Ross and I are doing an act together."

"Oh." Jeremy opened the door a little more. "Why didn't you say so?" He was wearing a black top hat and a cape.

"I'm the master of ceremonies for the show," Jeremy bragged. "I'm going to do a few jokes between acts."

"That's great," Ashley said. "Here's one for you. What wears a top hat and a cape and looks like a geek?"

Jeremy smirked. "Very funny," he said as he let her in.

Ashley followed Jeremy into the large old auditorium. The lights were dim at the back of the room, and Ashley had to squint at first to see what was happening.

"Ross is up there on the stage," Jeremy said. "Everybody's got a little space to practise in."

Ashley glanced around and saw groups of kids scattered all over the stage and in the orchestra seats.

Phoebe was standing halfway up the

19

aisle. She was petting Max Dorfman's white rabbit.

Ashley waved to Phoebe and hurried over to Ross.

"Hi," he said. "Where have you been?" He flashed her a smile.

Ashley's heart gave a little jump. "Sorry I'm late," she answered quickly. "I was waiting for Mary-Kate, but it turned out she isn't coming." She eyed the long black box that Ross had set up on a big table. "This is the magic box?" she asked. "What do I do?"

Ross bowed and gestured as if he were holding a car door open for her. "Hop in," he said.

Ashley gulped. The box looked complicated. From a distance, you couldn't tell that there was a secret compartment inside. But up close Ashley could see it.

And then Ashley spotted a gigantic saw lying on the floor. "You aren't going to use that – are you?" she squeaked.

"What's the matter?" Ross teased. "Don't think I can – cut it?"

He bent over and picked up the saw. "Doesn't it look real?" he asked. "It's actually totally harmless. The blade is made of rubber."

"Phew!" Ashley touched the rubber blade, just to make sure. "But seriously, how am I supposed to get in that box?"

"Like this." Ross flipped some latches and all the sides of the box folded down flat. Now it was easy for her to

slide in and lie down.

Ashley hopped up on the table and stretched out flat on her back. Then Ross closed the sides of the box around her and put the lid on top.

One end had two holes where her feet stuck out. The other end had a hole for her head.

The lid of the box and the sides were hinged together. In the middle of the box, near Ashley's waist, was a narrow slit just wide enough for the blade of a saw to fit through. At the slit, the box could be separated into two sections.

"Great," Ross said after he had locked her inside. "I'm going out for a pizza now. See you later!" He turned and started to walk away.

"Ross, don't you dare leave me in here!" Ashley called after him. She knew he was just kidding, but even the thought of being trapped in the box still made her really nervous.

"I'm just joking," Ross said, coming back and picking up the saw.

Ashley braced herself as he slid the saw down through the slit in the middle of the box. The rubber blade touched her stomach.

"If that was a real saw, you would have taken two inches off my waist," Ashley said.

"Right," Ross agreed. "I wanted you to see how this works. The saw needs to go all the way through the box. So before I cut you in half, you've got to get your body out of the way."

"How?" Ashley asked.

"Put your right hand on the bottom of the box," Ross said. "There's a little lever there. When you pull it, the bottom will slide open and another compartment will open up underneath you."

Ashley felt around for the lever. Yup – there it was. She gave it a yank.

"Whoa!" she cried.

The minute she pulled the lever, a portion of the box underneath her fell away – and her rear end dropped down about twelve inches. Her whole body jerked towards the centre of the box. Her chin hit one end of the wooden case, and her feet scraped against the top of the openings at the other end.

"Ow!" Ashley cried.

"Wait!" Ross said. "You weren't supposed to pull it yet."

"Great! Now you tell me!" Ashley groaned.

Ross opened all the latches and folded down the sides of the box again. Ashley hopped out.

"Look," he said. "I know this is tricky. My uncle said it will take some practice. But I'll be talking, so the audience won't notice you slipping down into the secret compartment. You also have to replace your real feet with fake feet."

"How will I do that?" Ashley asked.

Ross told Ashley how she'd get into the box and he'd close it up. Then he'd twirl the table around so the audience couldn't see her feet for a minute.

"Inside the box there will be two fake feet on long wooden poles," he told her. "All you do is pull your feet out of the holes at the end of the box. Then grab the long poles and stick the fake feet through the holes."

"Okay," Ashley said.

"I'll swing the table around again," Ross explained. "And you wiggle the fake

feet – on the poles – with your hands."

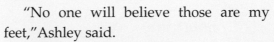

Ross held out a pair of fake feet with clunky shoes and socks on them. Two long rods extended out of the ankles. He gripped the handles and moved the feet back and forth.

"No one will believe those are my feet," Ashley said.

"Why not?" Ross asked.

"Because everyone knows I wouldn't be caught dead in those shoes," Ashley said.

"You can dress up the feet with whatever shoes you want," Ross explained. "Just as long as they match the shoes you're wearing that night."

Ashley shrugged. "Doesn't sound that complicated," she said.

"Want to give it a shot?" Ross asked.

They ran through the trick once. Ross locked up Ashley inside the box. Then he turned the table so that her feet faced away from the audience. Ross made up some patter while Ashley pulled her feet out of the holes. She grabbed the wooden poles and tried to stick the fake feet through, but she couldn't do it in time. When Ross turned the table around, there were no fake feet sticking out of the hole – and no real feet, either.

"Ashley, what happened?" Ross asked.

"I need more time to switch the feet," Ashley complained. "You've got to talk longer."

To be continued … go to page 32

Your future in your hands

Mary-Kate and Ashley know what they want from their futures. They want to go to college, act in and produce feature films, and continue to run their company. But what does your future hold? Here's a fun way to find out! Follow the pictures and see what your hands say about you.

Heart line
The heart line tells you all about your love style – romantic, fiery, practical, this line reveals all!

Sun line
This shows how successful you're likely to be in your career and how much money you stand to make!

Life line
This line shows whether you're an energetic, out and about type, or whether you prefer to chill out on the sofa with a stack of vidoes.

Marriage lines
Don't worry if you have two or three – these lines can also mean romances, rather than a march down the aisle!

Fate line
This can tell you about your future career and how many jobs you're likely to have.

Head line
Your head line doesn't show how smart you are, but it does show how you think and how you're likely to approach problems.

WHICH HAND DO I READ?
Usually palmists read whichever hand you write with. This is because that hand represents your conscious self, while the other hand represents your unconscious. So for a glimpse into the future, check out your homework-writing hand!

FunFact
Long fingers are a sign of artistic ability, so if that's you, grab a pad and start sketching!

Life line

The stronger and deeper this line is, the more likely it is that you love sports and all things action. Sometimes it will have little breaks in it. These breaks mean big changes in your life, such as starting at a new school. If the life line ends in a fork, it could mean that you'll eventually move far away from your home town, maybe even abroad! If you have any lines running alongside the life line, these mean you have bags of willpower.

Fate line

This line shows how focused (or not!) you can be when you try. If it starts close to your life line, your family will always be important to you. If it starts far away from the life line, you're imaginative and creative, and might end up in an unusual job! Breaks can indicate changes of direction, such as starting a new job when you're older. If the line is deep, it means you're a strong person who isn't easily put off. If it's light, it means you're an idealist who likes to go your own way.

Heart line

The heart line represents your emotional side. If it ends under your first finger (the one you point with), it means you're really emotional and should probably avoid weepy movies! If it ends between your first finger and the next one, you're a good balance of sensitive and practical. The more the line curves, the more sensitive you are, and if the line is deep, you'll move heaven and earth to be with the one you love!

Head line

Your head line shows how you work things out. If it starts high above the life line, it means you're independent and like to go your own way. If it starts with the lifeline, it shows that your family have a big influence on you. If it's tucked under the lifeline, you're a little on the shy side. A straight line means you like to know all the facts before you make a decision. If it curves downwards, you're dreamy and imaginative, and if it curves upwards you're the emotional type.

Marriage line

This line is tucked under your little finger. Lots of little lines mean lots of romances! If you have one line stronger than the others, that's your marriage line. The closer to your little finger it is, the older you'll be when you get married.

FunFact
Pointed fingers mean you love things to be beautiful all the time – you could be a designer, daahling!

Sun line

If you have a strong-looking sun line, you'd better open a bank account now for the big bucks you're going to make! Another sign to watch out for is a cross under your first finger, which could mean a lucky windfall.

FunFact
Short fingers mean you're practical and energetic – you're probably good with computers.

Fun facts about
Mary-Kate and Ashley
Did you know...

She has a dog called Jack that's part poodle and part Chihuahua – sounds interesting…

Mary-Kate has two horses. One's called CD and the other is called Star. She has ribbons and trophies that she's won in horse shows, and her first love was – you've guessed it – a horse! He was called Four by Four, and she still remembers him. Aww!

Her idea of a perfect day would include a quick jog along the beach, some serious shopping for loads of goodies, and then a relaxing massage….

Mary-Kate's favourite number? 8.

We know Mary-Kate loves Christmas, but her favourite part? It's going out to choose the tree, then decorating it with the whole family while listening to some Christmas music. Cool yule!

And her favourite actress? Mary-Kate really admires Cameron Diaz.

When she's at college, Mary-Kate fancies taking a cookery course so she can whip up a meal like mum makes. That way she won't feel too homesick!

When the sisters were younger they spent a lot of time on set making their movies. But it wasn't all work and no play! Mary-Kate had a favourite joke she liked to play, which involved secretly attaching a clothes peg to someone's clothes, then waiting to see how long it took them to notice. Some people went around all day wearing clothes pegs – they would go to lunch and even go home!

Want to know what Ashley really, really wants? A flat-screen TV! Maybe Santa will bring her one…

One of the highlights of Ashley's life was when she finally grew tall enough to go on all the rides at her local amusement park. Even big stars like the simple things in life!

Her fave fashion fix? Shoes, shoes, and shoes!

Ashley's idea of a perfect day would include a manicure, meeting friends for some grub and then spinning off to a yoga class.

Ask Ashley if she and Mary-Kate have ever tried to switch places to fool people and she'll say 'We haven't tried it.' But that's not what their mum says… maybe Ashley just, er, doesn't remember!

Ashley's favourite number? 8. (Hey, that's what Mary-Kate said! Must be one of those 'twin things'!)

And her fave actress? Ashley really rates Drew Barrymore, because she's an actress and producer.

Ashley has been known to nod off to sleep with the TV still on…zzz.

When she has time off from her hectic schedule, Ashley loves to curl up with a good book. She especially loves mysteries and historical fiction.

Anything she's proud of? 'Staying grounded while all this is going on around us.'

ashley

Mary-Kate and Ashley's
guide to your best sleepover ever!

Mary-Kate and Ashley love sleepovers. They're a great way to catch up with your mates, have some full-on heavy duty pampering (nails! hair! lip gloss!) and chow down on some double-yum snacks at the same time. But you can't just sling these things together, so here's a guide to having your best sleepover ever.

Q How many people should I invite?

A Sleepovers are all about keeping things small and cosy. Plus there's a limit to how many mates you can pack into your bedroom (unless you live in a castle!). You should aim to have a maximum of five friends over at one time. Six is plenty for a (small, cute 'n' cosy) pyjama party.

Q What's the best midnight munchies?

A Sleepovers are about having fun, so you should have some of your fave nibbles. How about:
- a selection of dips, such as humus and soft cheese, with tortillas, crisps and some sliced up raw carrots and celery for dipping.
- a tub of ice-cream, and maybe some chocolate cake or cookies.

Q What can we do?

A Here are a few things that are sure to make your sleepover go with a swing
- give each other a new hairstyle you've never tried before.
- put on your fave CD and make up a new dance routine you can show off to everyone at school.
- take turns painting each other's toenails – it's always tricky trying to do your own!
- experiment with make-up. After all, it's not as if you're going out anywhere!

Q What's the best thing to wear?

Pyjamas, of course! But what kind of jim-jams are your style?

A slinky satin-style.

B a cute, frilly nightie.

C an oversize T-shirt with a teddy bear on the front.

And your slippers?

A even your slippers have kitten heels!

B you've customised them so they're all lacy and sweet.

C they're the kind that look like stuffed animals.

Dressing gown?

A actually, yours is called a negligee and it's long and sooo sophisticated.

B it's made of towelling, just like the one you had when you were little.

C it's got a fur collar.

Sleepover secret
At the beginning of your sleepover, all make a pact that you'll keep any secrets that you tell each other.

Mostly A's
Wow, you're one dazzling diva! Even at a sleepover there's no way your style is going to slip. Just remember you're here to relax and have fun – let your immaculate hair down and relax!

Mostly B's
You're a real romantic, and you just love getting together with your friends to discuss fashion, guys, the latest hair trends, guys, make-up and – oh, yeah – guys!

Mostly C's
You have a crazy sense of humour and know how to make your mates curl up laughing. They know they're in for loads of fun when you all get together!

Mary-Kate and Ashley's
Dream Directory

So you've had fun with your sleepover. You stayed up late, you gossipped, you giggled, you grooved – and then, finally, you went to sleep. But do you remember what you dreamed about? Can dreams really tell the future, or do they tell you what your secret self is really thinking? Check out this guide to meanings, and dream on!

Bicycle
Dreaming about riding a bike is a sign that you have some seriously big decisions coming up. (Like maybe whether to go for the glitter body gel or the lippy when you go shopping!)

Cake
Oh, goodie! If you dream about a cake, it means you have some treats in store. Could be a party invite is winging its way to you.

Angels
If you dream about angels it's a good sign. You're going to be lucky in love, so hang out where the cute guy can see you – he's bound to notice you!

Eating
Dreams of eating and feasting mean that you're feeling contented and happy, and things will stay that way.

Flying
A dream about flying means that you're going to be successful in your endeavours. Scary test coming up at school? Bring it on – you'll fly through it!

Dancing
Dancing is associated with luck and prosperity, which sounds a lot like a rise in pocket money. Make sure you tell your parents about this one!

Garden
If you dream about being in a beautiful garden, it's a sign of both love and wealth to come – a great combination!

Heat
If you're feeling the heat in your dreams, it could be a sign that you're feeling a teeny bit worried. Anything bothering you at school or at home? Speak to your teacher or one of your parents.

Invisible
If you're invisible in your dream, watch out – someone might be about to discover your best-kept secret.

Jewellery

If you see jewellery in your dreams, this is a sign that someone is going to give you a great big present. Make it easy for them – leave a list lying around of things you'd like!

Key

If you dream about a key, this is symbolic of a mystery you want to solve. Keep persevering and you'll get there.

Ladder

A ladder looming into view means some totally unexpected good luck – you could find some money you didn't know you had tucked away in your pocket!

Makeup

If you dream about make-up, you secretly wonder how the rest of the world sees you. Lip gloss is fun, but remember, it's who you are underneath that really counts.

Needle

If you dream about a needle, it means that you're thinking hard about what you want to do when you're older. Don't worry, you have plenty of time to decide!

Ocean

A dream about a big ocean could mean that you're feeling a little bit overwhelmed by all the things in your life. Take some time out, have a long soak in a hot tub and relax.

Party

Dreaming you're at a party is a sign that you want to meet more people. Join an after-school club – you might make some new friends!

Queen

A dream about meeting a queen means that you're getting ready to make some changes in your life and let people know that you're not going to be pushed around.

Road

If a long road stretches ahead of you in your dream, you're wondering if you've made the right decision about something recently.

Shopping

If you're shopping, could be that you're feeling unfulfilled. Try a new hobby.

Teddy Bear

Dreaming about your favourite teddy? Don't worry, you're not turning into a baby, it just means you need a big hug. Mums and dads are usually pretty good for this!

Uniform

A dream about your school uniform means you're feeling a bit rebellious and want to stand out from the crowd. (On the plus side, a uniform does mean you never have to worry about what to wear!)

Volcano

Are your dreams full of erupting volcanoes? This means your mind and body need a little cleansing mini-spa. Listen to relaxing music, stock up on some aromatherapy oils and think calm thoughts.

Wind

Dreaming of struggling through windy weather can mean you're finding school or home life a bit of a struggle. Find a sympathetic friend or teacher to talk to.

Xmas

If you dream about Christmas, it's a good sign that you like your family, and could mean you'll be visiting a relative you don't often see.

Yelling

Yelling out loud in a dream means that you want to express yourself and let everyone know how you feel.

Zodiac

Dreaming about the signs of the zodiac means you want to know what's going to happen to you. Remember, nothing just happens – you make it happen!

Mary-Kate and Ashley's
guide to friendship

Mary-Kate and Ashley have each other to be best buddies with, and they know each other pretty well. You probably think you know your best friend just as well, but do you really? And what kind of a friend are you, anyway? See how you score in our friendship quiz!

What kind of a friend are you?

You accidentally discover your friend's deepest, darkest secret, and it's really *Eww!*. Do you

 A try to keep quiet but you can't resist a little whispering

 B surprise her with your new knowledge at the first opportunity

 C keep quiet, she's your best friend after all

Your friend 'fesses up: She's got a crush on the same guy *you* think is really cute, and she wants your advice on how to get his attention. Do you

 A tell everyone you know that she fancies him

 B tell her he already has a girlfriend, and secretly vow that he soon will – you!

 C take her shopping, give her a total makeover and help her find out where he hangs out

She's having a major homework crisis with a subject she hates, and she wants to copy yours. You

 A tease her like mad in front of your mates for not being able to keep up

B let her copy everything – provided she lends you that new CD for as long as you want

C try to encourage her to speak to the teacher

You go shopping together. She's got loads to spend and you're broke. She tries on an expensive combo that really doesn't suit her and asks how it looks. Do you

A fall about laughing, and can't wait to tell your other mates about it

B smile and say it's great; it may look awful on her, but it would look great on you and you can persuade her to let you borrow it

C spot something really cool and get her to try that on instead

Mostly A's

It's not that you don't care about your friend's feelings, it's just that you love to gossip! You can't keep a secret to save your life, and your friend better wise up – anything she tells you will probably be front page news!

Mostly B's

As friends go, you're the queen of mean! You always turn things to your own advantage and don't really care about your poor old mate at all! Beware – it won't be long before she finds out you're not a true friend!

Mostly C's

You are a Really Good Mate – you're there when she needs you and you're full of good advice. You and your friend should be best mates for life!

Now You See Him, Now You Don't

continued from page 21

"No, you've got to move faster," he insisted. "If I keep talking for too long, the audience will suspect something sneaky is going on."

Ashley sighed. She knew he was right, but it seemed impossible to go faster.

"Ashley, this is a great trick," Ross said. "No one will have a better trick than this. You've just got to practise, that's all."

They tried it again. And again. But they couldn't seem to get it right.

"What's the problem, Ashley?" Ross asked. He folded his arms. "It's not that hard."

Ashley frowned. "It is that hard," she argued. "We have to keep practising."

They tried the trick a few more times. But each time it seemed like Ross was talking faster and faster.

"Ross, slow down!" Ashley said. "You're not giving me enough time. Nobody could do the trick that quickly."

"I bet anyone else could," Ross said.

Ashley bit her lip and glared at Ross. "Why are you being so stubborn?" she asked.

"Me!" he cried, throwing up his hands. "You're the one who's being stubborn. Just like you always are."

Ashley gasped. "What?" she cried.

"Forget it," Ross said. "I'm getting out of here." He jumped off the stage and ran out of the auditorium. The heavy door slammed behind him.

Ashley stared after him. *I can't believe Ross and I have just had our first fight,* she thought. *Is our magic trick going to be okay?*

Are we going to be okay?

CHAPTER THREE

"I'll bet you five dollars," Elliot said. Mary-Kate turned to look at him as she slipped into her seat next to Jeremy in biology class.

Elliot sat across the aisle from her, one row back, at the end of a big lab table. Ross and some other guys were standing next to him.

"I'll bet five dollars my magic act gets more applause than Ross's," Elliot bragged with a grin.

Mary-Kate sighed. *Why does Elliot have to turn everything into a competition?* she wondered.

"You're on," Ross said, sticking out his hand to shake on the deal.

"Check this out." Elliot reached into his backpack and pulled out a rolled-up poster. He unrolled it to show to Ross and the other guys.

"I printed up a bunch of these yesterday while you were busy trying to saw your girlfriend in half," Elliot told them.

Mary-Kate gasped. The poster showed

a picture of a horse with the words DON'T MISS THE HIGHLIGHT OF THE MAGIC SHOW, SUGAR THE WONDER HORSE!

"I plastered them all over town yesterday," Elliot said. "Mary-Kate and I are going to blow everyone out of the water!"

Mary-Kate hurried over to Elliot. "Elliot, why did you do that?" she demanded in a low voice. "We should make sure the trick will work before we start advertising it!"

"What's the problem, Mary-Kate?" Elliot asked. "You told me you could make Sugar do magic tricks. You said you had a plan."

"I do," Mary-Kate replied. "Sugar's a great horse, and I know I can train him. But he's not mine. I need to ask permission to borrow him for the show."

"So ask," Elliot said. "I'm sure the owner will say yes. The show's for charity – everybody in town supports it."

"I was planning to go to the stable this afternoon and ask," Mary-Kate said. "But I also have to figure out how to bring the horse into the auditorium—"

"I'll ask the headmaster for special permission," Elliot said. "Don't worry, Mary-Kate. It'll all work out."

Mr. Barber, the biology teacher, entered the room. "Let's take our seats, people," he bellowed.

Mary-Kate hurried back to her seat. Mr. Barber's head was bald on top and fringed with shaggy grey hair. He wore wire-rimmed glasses and a zip-up jacket. Jeremy leaned towards Mary-Kate as Mr. Barber unzipped his jacket.

"Let's see if he keeps the record going," Jeremy whispered.

Mr. Barber was famous at Harrington for wearing the same tie – a loud, goofy, extra-wide tie swirled with orange, red, blue, and purple – every single day. Every day for the last thirty years.

"Will we be seeing the tie again today?" Jeremy murmured like a sports announcer. "Can Mr. Barber keep up his record?"

Mr. Barber pulled his jacket off. There was the tie.

"Yes!" Jeremy whispered. "The record grows!"

Mary-Kate giggled at her cousin.

While the class settled down, Mr. Barber said, "I have to go to the main office for a few minutes. I want all of you to pair off and study quietly for the quiz on the digestive system." He left the room.

"Mary-Kate!" Elliot called in a loud whisper. "Study with me."

Jeremy pursed his lips and made sloppy kissing noises. Mary-Kate jabbed her cousin with her elbow. "Stop being a pain," she whispered. Then she took a seat next to Elliot at the lab table.

"I'll quiz you first," Mary-Kate said.

"Forget the quiz," Elliot said. "We need to talk about our trick for the magic show. Let's hear your plan."

Mary-Kate nodded excitedly. She'd gone to the library and read a few magic books. She'd found a great trick that they could use with a horse.

"It's a card trick," she explained. "You tell me to pick a card, and I'll

pick one out of the deck. You won't be able to see it because you'll be blindfolded. After I pick the card, I'll show it to the audience – and to Sugar. Then I'll put it back in the deck and take the blindfold off you."

Elliot nodded. "A card trick – I love it. Go on."

"You shuffle the deck and do some hocus-pocus," Mary-Kate said. "Pretty soon you say 'I think I've found your card,' and you show it to me."

"I think I know this trick," Elliot said. "But where does the horse come in?"

"I'll say 'Why don't you ask the horse if it's the right card?' Then Sugar will nod his head yes when you show him the card!"

"Brilliant!" Elliot said. "But how can you train a horse to recognize fifty-two different cards?"

Mary-Kate smiled and lowered her voice to a really soft whisper. "I can't. That's part of the trick."

"What do you mean?" Elliot asked.

"I'll train him to nod his head yes if you hold up the card with your left hand," Mary-Kate explained. "I know Sugar can do it. I once trained a horse to do something like this, and he wasn't as smart as Sugar is."

"Mary-Kate, this trick is going to be even better than I thought!" Elliot said. "I know another trick we can add to this one – it will really get the crowd going. I'll show Sugar the wrong card two or three

times at first – on purpose. Then, finally, I'll pull the right card out of a sealed envelope. The horse will nod yes. Then I'll hold the card up to the audience. They'll go wild!"

"But, Elliot, how do you get the right card into the sealed envelope?" Mary-Kate asked.

Elliot pretended to lock his lips. "I'll never tell," he said, his eyes dancing. "Magicians' secret."

"Excellent," Mary-Kate said. "I'll just teach Sugar to shake his head no if you hold up the card with your right hand. Now we just have to figure out how to get Sugar on stage."

"I'll try and get permission from the Harrington headmaster today," Elliot told her.

Mary-Kate nodded. "And I'll ask my friend at the stables if I can borrow Sugar."

"Right," Elliot agreed. "When you get to the auditorium, there's a back door behind the stage. We can lead the horse in through the door and up a ramp to the stage."

"I think it might work!" Mary-Kate cheered. "This is going to be awesome. We'll have one of the best tricks in the show!"

As soon as class was over, Mary-Kate rushed over to Ashley. "I've got to tell you about the trick I'm doing with Elliot," she said.

Ashley gathered up her books and they started to walk out of the door. "I hope he's not sawing you in half," she grumbled. "Believe me, it's not as easy as it looks."

"No – we're doing a card trick,"

Mary-Kate whispered. "And I'm going to train Sugar to recognise the card!"

"You're kidding!" Ashley said. "You guys are using a horse in your trick?"

"Yup," Mary-Kate said. "But first I've got to talk Sean into letting me borrow Sugar for the show. Can you come with me to the stables this afternoon? We can go riding for a little while, too."

Ashley shook her head. "No way. You know me and horses."

"But it would be soooo much fun to go riding together," Mary-Kate said. "It'll be like our own special sister time."

Ashley hesitated. "Well . . ." she began.

"Pretty please?" Mary-Kate said sweetly.

"I guess it could be fun," Ashley said. "But you'd better make sure I don't have any problems with that horse!"

"Don't worry," Mary-Kate said. "I'll make sure everything goes perfectly."

Sean waved as he walked towards Mary-Kate at the stables later that day.

"Hi, Sean." Mary-Kate waved back. "This is my sister, Ashley."

"Hi," Ashley said. She jumped as a horse flicked her with his tail.

"I have a couple of favours to ask," Mary-Kate went on.

Sean raised his eyebrows. "What's up?"

"I was wondering if I could borrow one of your horses for a magic trick I'm doing in the Harrington magic show," Mary-Kate asked.

Sean listened while she told him all about the show and the card trick she and Elliot wanted to do.

"That sounds really cool," Sean said. "I'll check with my dad, but I think it'll be okay."

"Great, thanks!" Mary-Kate said.

"What's the second favour?" Sean asked.

"I was wondering if Ashley could ride with me today," Mary-Kate said.

"Sure." Sean headed into the stables. He walked down the row of horses. "Let's see. Which horse would be good for her?"

"Got any of the kind that rocks back and forth?" Ashley asked.

Mary-Kate giggled. "You're going to love Sugar," she told her sister. She turned to Sean. "Can Ashley ride him today?"

Sean stared at Mary-Kate. "Sugar?" he said. "Are you sure you want me to get Sugar for you?"

"Yeah, why?" Mary-Kate asked, confused. "He's a great horse."

"You must be a really good rider," Sean said with a whistle. "I'll go saddle him up for you."

"Why is he saying that, Mary-Kate?" Ashley demanded as Sean walked away. Mary-Kate could tell she was getting nervous.

"I'm not sure," Mary-Kate said as they walked outside. "But would I let you get on an unsafe horse?"

"I hope not!" Ashley said as Sean headed towards them. He was leading a beautiful grey horse with a white patch on his right ankle. He also led a dappled brown horse towards Mary-Kate.

"This one's name is Chestnut," Sean said. "I thought you would have fun riding him, Mary-Kate."

He tied both horses to a fence, then started to walk away. "Will you guys be okay if I leave?" Sean called over his shoulder.

"Definitely," Mary-Kate said.

"Maybe," Ashley squeaked.

"Don't worry," Mary-Kate reassured her sister. "They wouldn't call him Sugar if he wasn't so sweet!"

Mary-Kate took Sugar's reins and held them for Ashley. "Climb on up!"

Ashley put her foot in the stirrup and heaved herself into the saddle. She clung to the horse's neck with both hands.

"Okay, take the reins," Mary-Kate said, handing them to her sister.

Ashley slowly reached forward. But just as she was about to grab the reins, Sugar started backing up and shaking his mane.

"Mary-Kate!" Ashley shrieked.

"Whoa!" Mary-Kate called, trying to steady the horse. She petted the horse's side.

Sugar whinnied. He pulled away and started to back up faster.

"I'm going to fall!" Ashley cried. She buried her face in the horse's neck as she held on. "Hellllp!"

Mary-Kate caught up with Sugar and grabbed the reins. She pulled hard enough to get Sugar's attention.

"Whoa, boy. Steady," she said firmly. The horse settled down a bit.

"Climb down, Ashley," Mary-Kate directed.

Ashley jumped off the horse. "Sweet?

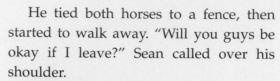

Well-behaved?" she yelled at her sister. "Mary-Kate has the horse smell gone to your head?"

"I don't get it!" Mary-Kate said. "He was perfect the last time I rode him. Let me try."

She climbed onto Sugar's back. But as soon as she was seated, he started backing up again.

"Whoa!" Mary-Kate said. "Steady!"

Sugar calmed down. "Okay, now, boy," Mary-Kate said, stroking his neck. "Let's go for a walk around the corral."

She clicked her tongue and gave the signal for Sugar to start walking. But he wouldn't move. No matter what she did, he stood perfectly still.

"Well, at least it's not me," Ashley commented.

"I don't understand it," Mary-Kate said, climbing down. "I know this is the horse I rode the last time. He looks the same, but he's acting so different . . ."

Mary-Kate tied Sugar to the fence and sat down on the grass. "Ashley, how am I going to teach Sugar to nod yes or no when I can't even get him to walk?" she asked.

"Magic?" Ashley suggested weakly.

From the corner of her eye Mary-Kate could see Sean strolling towards them.

"What's the trouble?" Sean asked, walking up to them.

"Sugar isn't behaving as well as I thought he would," Mary-Kate said. "I can't get him to move an inch. Are you sure this is Sugar?"

"It's Sugar all right," Sean said with a nod. "I'm not surprised he won't obey you. He's so stubborn that most people can't even get him out of his stable."

But how can that be? Mary-Kate thought. *He was so good the last time I rode him.*

"How am I going to train him for the magic show?" she wondered out loud.

"Do you have to do a horse trick?" Ashley asked. "Why don't you and Elliot do something else?"

"We can't," Mary-Kate groaned. "Elliot already plastered the town with posters about Sugar the Wonder Horse. Everyone will be expecting to see him!"

Ashley put her arm around Mary-Kate's shoulders. "I hate to say it, but if that's the horse you want to train, you're in big trouble."

CHAPTER FOUR

"Oh, Ashley," Phoebe gushed. "Don't you think he's the cutest thing you've ever seen?"

"Hmm?" Ashley asked. It was Saturday, and she and Phoebe were riding the shuttle bus into the small town near White Oak Academy. Ashley looked up from a book she had borrowed from Phoebe. It was a book of magic tricks, and Ashley was reading about how to cut a rope in half and then make it whole again.

Ashley leaned over Phoebe and glanced out of the window of the shuttle bus. "Who's cute? Who are we looking at?"

"Not out there," Phoebe said. "I was talking about the rabbit Max is using in our act."

Ashley turned to face her friend. "You've been talking about that rabbit all week," she said.

"I can't help it," Phoebe said. She leaned back on the brown leather seat. "I've never had a pet before. Besides, you've been talking about magic all week!"

"I know!" Ashley said. "I'm totally into it now." She'd been reading up on magic partly for fun – and partly because she was worried. She really wanted to get Ross's trick right at practice that afternoon. That way they wouldn't fight again.

The bus pulled onto Main Street. Ashley closed the book and put it in her tote bag.

"You know, Ashley," Phoebe said, buttoning her pea coat, "that poor bunny doesn't even have a name. Don't you think we should give him one?"

"Definitely," Ashley agreed. "Max bought him from the pet shop a week ago. Why hasn't he named him yet?"

"I don't know," Phoebe said. "Maybe because he doesn't love the rabbit as much as I do." She paused, thinking of names. "What about Dickinson? After Emily Dickinson?"

"Dickinson?" Ashley rolled her eyes. They had an Emily Dickinson poster hanging in their room. She was Phoebe's favorite poet. "Isn't that a little sophisticated for a rabbit?"

To be continued … go to page 46

Mary-Kate and Ashley's
guide to looking good

On set, Mary-Kate and Ashley have stylists to make sure they look their best, but at home, they're on their own, just like you! So here are some tips from the top on looking good and feeling great!

How much do you know about looking good?
Take this fun quiz and find out your gorgeousness rating.

1 Your idea of a perfect lunch is:

a) chips, chips, chips!
b) a tuna sandwich with a yogurt and an apple.
c) burgers – but you have a salad, too.

2 Your make-up collection consists of:

a) what make-up collection?
b) a full kit, plus brushes, in a special bag.
c) a couple of pots of lippy rolling around in the back of a drawer.

3 'Fess up: you go to bed without washing your face and cleaning your teeth:

a) whenever you're too tired to bother.
b) never ever *ever*!
c) once or twice after a late night, but you're not proud of it.

4 Your nails are:

a) a bit nibbled-at and could probably do with a scrub.
b) almond shaped and perfectly manicured.
c) you do wear varnish sometimes, but it sometimes gets chipped.

5 Your hair:

a) goes its own way.
b) is washed every day and does what you tell it to.
c) you love trying different styles when you get the chance.

6 Your ideal day out is:

a) going for a milkshake and burger with your mates.
b) shopping!
c) pizza and a movie.

Mostly a's

Wow! Junk food, bad habits… you have a lot to learn about how to look and feel your best. But don't worry, you've come to the right place! Read on for lots of tips to buff up your cuteness rating.

Mostly b's

You know all about looking after your skin, hair and health, and know your way around a make-up bag, but there's always something more to learn, so see what tips you can pick up here!

Mostly c's

You like fashion and love to try different styles, but you don't always have the time to look your best. Find out how to make looking good part of your daily routine, guaranteed fuss-free.

Party hair

Try new styles from fashion magazines

*

Add a glitter clasp for extra glamour

*

Use a smoothing conditioner for super shine

Classroom cutie

Look a classroom cutie by following a few simple rules.

* Keep hair simple. Try scrunchies and bobbles with ponytails, bunches or plaits.
* A slick of clear gloss on your lips will make you feel you're still groovy.
* Keep nails neat and pretty, and use a clear gloss that won't show the chips.
* Classroom princesses always brush their teeth thoroughly after meals!

Party face

Use a shimmery eye shadow

*

Slick on some blusher to highlight your cheekbones

*

Go wild with some glitter mascara

Weekend style

Try these fun looks for hanging out with friends at the weekend.

* Try some coloured lip gloss for extra weekend pizzazz.
* Try a little clear mascara to lengthen lashes – then find someone to flutter them at!
* A sweep of natural-looking blusher will give you a healthy glow – just don't overdo it!
* Do something a little different with your hair. Even just changing the parting can make a difference!

Beauty basics

* Lip gloss is much better than lipstick – it's lighter and fresher.
* If you overdo blusher, take it off and start again.
* Don't share eye make-up with even your best mates!
* A French manicure looks funky and fab.
* A light conditioner means you'll be able to tackle tangles without harming your hair!
* Ordinary soap is too drying, so use a soap or cleanser specially made for faces.
* Gently smudge an eye pencil under your lashes for a mysterious look!
* A pot of body glitter is great for instant sparkle.

Party looks

Check out some cool crystal tattoos

*

Or a glittery body gel

*

Or go for shine 'n' shimmer gel

Mary-Kate and Ashley's
guide to parties!

Great parties don't just happen. You have to make them happen!
Read on to find out how to lay on your best bash ever...

Stop right there!
Make sure your folks are happy with what you're planning –
having them coming home to find you're halfway through
a party they didn't know about is so not cool!

Are you a party animal?

Do you groove away on the dancefloor, or hide away
in the kitchen? Take this quick quiz and find out.

At a karaoke party

a you're first up – you love being the centre of
attention.

b nothing, but nothing, would get you up there!

c you're up for it if a couple of your mates will
join in to sing along to your fave girl band.

At a fancy dress party, you go as

a your favourite star.

b Snow White.

c you and your mate go as two parts of a
pantomime horse.

Your ideal party is

a dancing, music and action with absolutely
everyone you know there.

b you really prefer sleepovers with just a few friends.

c a beach barbie, so you can have some seaside fun.

What do you like best about parties?

a dancing to the latest sounds with cute guys.

b gossiping with your friends about who's wearing what
and who's seeing who.

c definitely the food!

**Who would you most like to go to
a party with?**

a a boy band.

b your favourite solo star.

c your favourite comedian.

Mostly a's
Wow, you're a real party animal! You love to glitz it
up and you have loads of style. In fact you're
probably planning your next party right now, so
read this guide before you do another thing!

Mostly b's
You like a party as much as the next
person, but you prefer to keep them
small. If you're organising anything,
you'll pay lots of attention to the
little details and make sure everyone
has a great time.

Mostly c's
The best thing about parties for
you is having a good laugh with
your mates. Any party you
organise will be loads of fun,
with some really good grub laid
on to keep everyone happy.

Sunday	Monday	Tuesday	Wednesday	Thursday	Friday	Saturday
June  THE PARTY IS ON!!!				1 Decide where to have party	2	
3	4	5	6	7 Send out invitations	8	9 PLAN THE FOOD
10	11	12	13 Organise music – check out CDs	14 Shop ahead for cold drinks	15	16
17	18	19	20 Decide on some cool party games	21	22	23 30 PARTY TIME
24	25	26	27	28	29	

Party tip

Get a friend to help you get everything ready – you'll have half the work and twice the fun!

Party tip

Help with the cleaning up afterwards. That way your folks won't mind when you want to throw another party!

Party Dos

Make sure you know how many guests are coming so you can organise food and drinks.

Move furniture up against the walls to give room to dance.

Mingle with your guests and make sure they're having fun.

Set a finish time, so everyone knows when the party's over!

Party Don'ts

Wait until the day before the party to send out the invites!

Have the lights on too bright – it's a real killer for atmosphere.

Ignore anyone – get everyone to join in the fun.

Make so much noise that the neighbours complain – have fun, but keep a lid on things!

Groovy grub

Stuck on what to serve? Here's some ideas.

Breadsticks, crisps and dips

Pizza slices

Chicken pieces

Veggie kebabs

Rolls with interesting fillings

Sausage rolls – everyone's fave

Don't forget some sweet treats

Mix fruit juice with sparkling mineral water for a different drink

How well do you know
Mary-Kate and Ashley?

Ever wondered what it would be like if Mary-Kate and Ashley really were your best friends? Then you'd know all about them! Well, take this quiz and find out just how well you know them already. Score two points for every question you get right.

1 You're choosing a birthday card to send to Mary-Kate and Ashley. You know Ashley is older than Mary-Kate, but by how long?

A two minutes **B** ten minutes **C** forty minutes

2 In Two of a Kind Mary-Kate and Ashley keep their own first names, but what are their characters' surnames?

A Burke **B** Brown **C** Black

3 You're going to visit the American city that Two of a Kind is set in. Which city does it say on your ticket?

A New York **B** Chicago **C** Detroit

4 You're going round to Mary-Kate and Ashley's and they introduce you to their family. What's the name of their older brother?

A Trent **B** Brent **C** Kent

5 Mary-Kate and Ashley are coming to your place to chill out and watch some TV. Which of these shows is their special favourite?

A Frasier   **B** Friends   **C** ER

6 You're going to hit the mall with Mary-Kate and Ashley for some serious shopping! Which kind of shoes do both girls prefer?

A kitten heels   **B** stiletto heels   **C** flip-flops

7 Mary-Kate and Ashley have invited you to spend their favourite holiday with them. Does this mean you'll be with them for

A Hallowe'en   **B** Christmas   **C** Thanksgiving

8 Mary-Kate and Ashley are telling you all about how they got started in showbiz. How old were they when their mum took them to an audition?

A 6 weeks   **B** 7 months   **C** 12 months

9 Ashley's telling you all about her time at school. Her favourite subject was

A maths   **B** science   **C** drama

10 Mary-Kate tells you her favourite school subject was

A history   **B** English   **C** art

Answers

1 (a) ✓ Ashley is two minutes older than Mary-Kate.
2 (a) ✓ Burke
3 (b) ✓ Chicago
4 (a) ✓ The girls' big bro is called Trent.
5 (b) ✓ Mary-Kate and Ashley both love Friends.
6 (c) ✓ Both girls are crazy about flip-flops!
7 (b) ✓ Christmas is the favourite holiday in the Olsen household.
8 (b) ✓ They were 7 months old when they joined a modelling agency.
9 (a) ✓ Ashley is nuts about maths!
10 (b) ✓ Mary-Kate loves English.

How did you score?

Under 8

The bad news is, you don't know as much as you thought about the real Mary-Kate and Ashley. The good news is there are lots of movies starring your faves to catch up on, so go on, get some popcorn, invite your mates around and have a real Mary-Kate and Ashley movie-fest!

10 -16

Seems like you know the girls pretty well already! If you want to find out even more, check out some of their books – great to curl up with in a cosy armchair!

Over 16

Congratulations! You know as much about Mary-Kate and Ashley as you do about your best friend! Look out for the latest Mary-Kate and Ashley buzz on their website at www.mary-kateandashley.com - don't forget to ask your folks' permission before you log on!

Now You See Him, Now You Don't

continued from page 37

"Well, we can't call him Emily, because he's a boy. And I don't want to name him after Shakespeare," Phoebe said. Phoebe loved William Shakespeare's plays and sonnets. "I'm saving that for a dog – if my parents ever let me get one."

"Where is Max keeping the rabbit?" Ashley asked. "I thought Harrington didn't allow pets in the dorms."

"They don't. Max has been trying to hide him, but he says it's getting too hard," Phoebe said. She gave Ashley a big smile. "That's why I've offered to keep him in our room."

"What? Hel-lo!" Ashley cried. "Phoebe, White Oak doesn't allow pets in the dorms either."

"Don't think of him as a bunny," Phoebe reasoned. "We can pretend he's – a slipper!"

Ashley groaned under her breath. "Is there any way I'm going to change your mind?" she asked.

Phoebe shook her head. "Don't worry, Ashley. No one will ever know he's there. I'll keep him safe and sound."

"Okay," Ashley said. "But be careful, because if Ms. Viola finds out she's going to be really mad!" Ms. Viola was the housemother at Porter House.

The bus pulled into the stop and the girls climbed off. They were standing on the town's main street in front of a row of shops and cafés. A brisk, cold wind blew up the street. Ashley put on her white knitted cap and started walking.

"Where should we go first?" Phoebe asked.

"How about the craft shop?" Ashley answered. "I want to get some sequins for my costume." She planned to wear a glamorous, sparkly outfit on stage, just like she'd seen in magic shows on TV.

"Look!" Phoebe cried. She pointed to a shopfront a few buildings down. "They're having a sale at Winnie's! Can we go there first?"

Ashley knew this was Phoebe's favourite thrift shop. Half her wardrobe was filled with old corduroy trousers, wild 1960s blouses, beaded 1930s dresses, and crazy fur hats. And the great thing was, she could put them all together and look amazing!

Phoebe stopped to gaze in the front window. "Maybe they've got some new vintage," she said excitedly.

"New vintage? Isn't that impossible?" Ashley teased.

Phoebe ignored her. "Wow – check out that fur-trimmed sweater!" she exclaimed, as they slipped into the warm shop. "I've got to try it on."

Ashley wandered around the thrift shop while Phoebe tried on the sweater. Most of the clothes weren't Ashley's taste. But there were some cool old necklaces and earrings in a display case.

"Hey, Ashley, look!" Phoebe called out. "Isn't that Mr. Barber's tie over there?"

Ashley turned round. "Hey, it is!" she said. "Who would have thought they'd make two of those hideous things?"

Phoebe walked over and picked up the bright swirly tie. It was identical to the tie Mr. Barber wore to school every day.

"It must be from the sixties," Phoebe said, tilting her head and studying it. "It has that pop art look."

"It's making my eyes pop!" Ashley said.

"Want to buy it?" Phoebe asked. "We could get one of the guys to wear it to class as a joke."

"I only have enough money to buy my costume decorations," Ashley said.

She looked at the tie again. Then she thought of the magic trick she had read about on the bus – how to cut a rope in half and make it whole again.

"I'd love to use that tie in a magic trick," Ashley said. She didn't have to use a rope for that trick. A tie would work just as well.

"But I thought Ross was sawing you in half," Phoebe said.

"He is," Ashley agreed, hesitating a little. "But we're having trouble with it. Maybe we should have a backup if it doesn't work out. And even if it does, two tricks are better than one." She explained the rope trick to Phoebe.

"That's a funny idea – especially if you can get Mr. Barber to go along with it," Phoebe said. "Why don't you buy the tie? It's not expensive. I'll lend you the money."

"Thanks," Ashley replied.

Phoebe bought the fur-trimmed sweater and the tie, and the girls hurried down the street to the craft shop.

"I need a glamorous costume for the show," Ashley explained. "So I'm going to sew sequins to a black leotard I have."

When they reached the shop, she went through the little boxes of sequins and shiny beads along the counter and picked some out.

Phoebe looked at her watch. "We've got to hurry. Rehearsal for the show starts in half an hour."

Ashley paid for her sequins and the girls hurried to the shuttle bus. They got off at Harrington's campus instead of at White Oak.

The door to the auditorium was locked again, but after a few loud knocks, Jeremy opened the door.

"What's the secret password?" he asked them.

"Dorkface?" Ashley guessed.

"Dorkface *is* the password!" he said, letting them by. "How did you know?"

Ashley didn't answer. She said goodbye to Phoebe and rushed to the back of the stage. Ross was there waiting for her.

"Hey," she called, slipping out of her jacket and hat. She glanced at him, wondering if he was still mad at her.

"Hey," Ross replied. "We have to work really hard today. I'm starting to get freaked that we won't have our trick ready. We've got only a week until the show."

Ashley nodded. She could sense the tension between them. They'd never

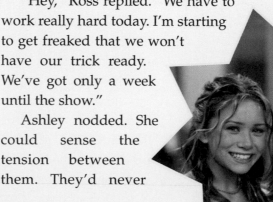

really made up since their fight.

For the next two hours Ashley tried her best to get into the secret compartment quickly. But each time Ross put the saw into the slot and pretended to cut her in half, she felt it hit her stomach.

"Come on, Ross," Ashley said. "You have to give me more time."

Ross looked at his watch. Ashley knew it was late. All the other students had already left the auditorium. She and Ross were the only ones left rehearsing.

"I'm talking for as long as I can." Ross frowned. "Maybe if you got in the box the way I told you to, we wouldn't have a problem."

"Maybe if you gave me better instructions, I would know what I'm doing," Ashley shot back. She paused, rubbing her forehead. *We've got to stop this arguing*, she thought. *I don't want to get into another fight.*

"Why don't I just practise by myself for a while?" Ashley suggested.

"Fine," Ross said. He walked off the stage and up the aisle. Then he left the auditorium and shut the door. Ashley stood on the stage, all alone in the auditorium.

"Fine," Ashley repeated. She began to calm down. Without Ross there, it was better. Ashley didn't feel so pressured. She could take her time to figure things out.

She started from the beginning. She climbed into the box and pulled the lid shut. She put her feet through the holes in the end. Then she practised pulling them out and switching the fake feet as fast as she could.

Yes! Ashley thought. This time she did it in about ten seconds. *Wait until I tell Ross.*

Ashley pushed on the top of the box to climb out. But the lid didn't budge.

"Come on," she grumbled. "Open!"

She gave another hard shove against the lid. It didn't move.

"Hey! Let me out of here," she called, banging on the box again from all sides. She tried to push open the sides, and then the top again.

It was no use. The box wouldn't open. She was trapped!

CHAPTER FIVE

"Help!" Ashley yelled as loud as she could. "Hellllp!"

She banged on the box a few more times in desperation. But it was no use. The box was locked. She was stuck.

What am I going to do now? she thought miserably.

"Ashley?" a voice called.

"Ross?" Ashley turned her head. "Ross! Get me out of here!"

Ross leaped onto the stage and unlocked the box. "I was on my way back to my dorm when I remembered that you couldn't unlock the box. So I ran all the way back here as fast as I could to get you out!"

Ashley jumped out of the box and shook her legs. It felt good to be able to move again. "I'm glad you remembered," she said. "I thought I was going to spend the night in that thing!"

Ross looked down at his trainers. "I'm sorry, Ashley. And I'm sorry I got annoyed with you before."

"I'm sorry, too," Ashley said. "I know you just want the trick to be good."

"And I know you were trying your best," Ross admitted. "You were right – I need to give you a little more time."

They smiled at each other. The tension between them melted away. "Let's not fight any more," Ashley said.

"Deal," Ross agreed. He grabbed her hand and held it for a second.

I can't believe we let such a silly thing come between us, Ashley thought. Then she remembered the rope trick.

"I came up with another trick, you know," Ashley said. "In case we couldn't get the box trick right."

"I'm sure we'll get it right eventually," Ross said. "But what's your idea for the other trick?"

"Well, I read about this magic trick where you cut a rope in half and then put it back together," she explained. "The catch is that you need two pieces of rope that look identical."

"A rope trick?" Ross asked.

"Not exactly," Ashley said, grinning. "You know that tie Mr. Barber wears every day?"

Ross nodded. "The eye-popper? How could I miss it?"

"I bought one exactly like it at the thrift shop in town," she said. "What if I pretended to cut Mr. Barber's tie in half instead of a rope?"

Ross laughed. "Mr. Barber will flip out. His students will love it!"

Ashley laughed, too. "No kidding. It

would be really funny."

"You know, Ashley," Ross said. "I'm sure the box trick is going to work – and it will be great. But that tie trick is hilarious. Why don't we do both tricks? Then our act will really rock!"

"All right," Ashley agreed. "I'll practise it in my room until I get it down perfectly."

Ross held Ashley's hand as they left the auditorium. She was so glad they'd made up. But in the back of her mind, there was still one thing that worried her.

She still hadn't mastered the box trick. And she hadn't even tried the tie trick yet.

The show is only a week away, she thought. *Will I be able to pull off both tricks in time?*

CHAPTER SIX

"So, did Ross like the tie trick?" Mary-Kate asked Ashley. The sisters were standing in the exercise ring at the Starbright Stables, waiting for Sean to bring Sugar out. Ashley was going to help Mary-Kate train Sugar.

"He loved it," Ashley said. "We're going to add it to our act. This afternoon I asked Mr. Barber if he wanted to be part of the act."

"Did he say yes?" Mary-Kate asked. She rubbed her mittened hands together in the chilly air.

To be continued ... go to page 56

To be continued ... go to page 56

Mary-Kate and Ashley's
guide to families

You can choose your friends, but when it comes to families, you're stuck with what you've got! So here's all you need to know about families.

The fairy tale family?

You think your family's quirky? Hey, even fairy tale families can give each othera bad time! Try this fun quiz then check out your score.

1 *You're Cinderella and your stepmum has forbidden you to go to the ball. Do you:*

a) Raid the wardrobes for something snazzy, then hitch a ride on a passing pumpkin. Nothing stops you getting your own way!

b) Send a message to your fairy godma – when your family fails, you need your mates!

c) Stay in and shell some peas. No one understands you around here!

2 *You're Snow White and your stepmum is spending ages with the magic mirror.* **Do You:**

a) Get the mirror to tell her you're way more gorgeous.

b) Lure her away with a treat – try a nice, juicy apple.

c) Run off to the woods in a sulk with seven short guys who think you're cool.

3 *You're Red Riding Hood, and your mum asks you to nip over to your gran's with a basket of goodies.*

a) Is she crazy – there are wolves out there!

b) Say you'll go with a friend. You and your bestie are enough to scare off any wolf!

c) Yell 'You don't care about me really!' and storm off. It'll serve everyone right if you get eaten!

Top tips for happy families

Family fact

Mary-Kate and Ashley have a brother, Trent, a little sister, Elizabeth, and a brother and sister, Taylor and Jake, from Dad's second marriage.

- Everyone has rows! When your family is having a spat, try not to take sides, and don't get upset; they'll sort it out eventually.

- Be considerate – clear your clobber from rooms the whole family shares and encourage the rest of the crew to do the same.

- Make sure everyone gets to watch their special fave TV programme each week.

- Get everyone to help with chores. If it's your turn to wash up, no excuses!

- Take turns! Whether it's playing CDs or using the computer, don't hog everything yourself.

- Bring your mum and/or dad breakfast in bed!

- Be ready to share your stuff. It makes things easier all round.

- Give everyone a great big hug – they're your family and you love 'em!

Mostly a's

Here's one girl who really knows how to get her own way! Never mind what anyone else thinks, as long as you get to do what you want, you're happy. You might need to think about others every now and then – parents are people, too!

Mostly b's

You know family life isn't always plain sailing, and you're prepared to compromise sometimes. If all else fails, you've always got your friends to rely on. Your family is great, but you don't expect them to be perfect – well, not all the time, anyway!

Mostly c's

Oh, dear, you can be a bit of a drama queen! Sometimes it can seem as if the whole family is ganging up to give you a hard time, but they probably just don't know how you really feel. Instead of throwing a moody, try talking to them – you could be surprised at how helpful they can be.

Family fact

Mary-Kate and Ashley say that, in their family, everyone shares their stuff – but you have to ask first!

Three reasons why you love 'em...

When the chips are down, they rally round and support you

Big brothers may tease you, but they sometimes have cool-looking friends they bring home...

When you're feeling blue, your mum fixes your favourite supper and everything looks a little bit better

... and three reasons why you (sometimes!) don't

Your big bruv thinks he's Grand Master of the remote control

Your sister *never* gets off the phone

Someone else always snaffles the last choccie biccie from the tin

Mary-Kate and Ashley's
Word Searches

Here are two wicked wordsearches for you to try! Use the lists and tick off each word as you find it. Remember, the words can go up, down, forwards, backwards – even diagonally! And each letter can be used more than once.

This one has hidden in it loads of things that you and Mary-Kate and Ashley love. See how many you can find!

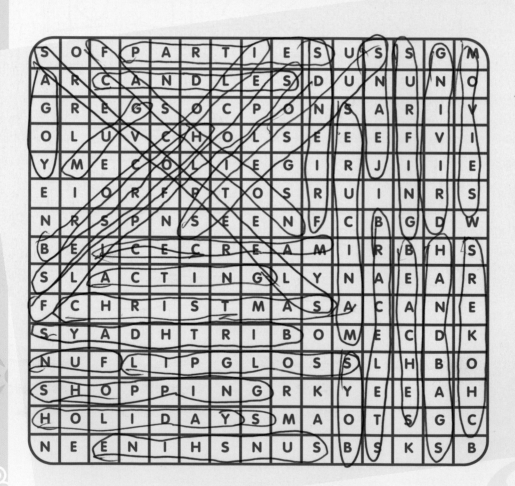

S	O	F	P	A	R	T	I	E	S	U	S	S	G	M
A	R	C	A	N	D	L	E	S	D	U	N	U	N	O
G	R	E	G	S	O	C	P	O	N	S	A	R	I	V
O	L	U	V	C	H	O	L	S	E	E	E	F	V	I
Y	M	E	C	O	L	I	E	G	I	R	J	I	I	E
E	I	O	R	F	P	T	O	S	R	U	I	N	R	S
N	R	S	P	N	S	E	E	N	F	C	B	G	D	W
B	E	I	C	E	C	R	E	A	M	I	R	B	H	S
S	L	A	C	T	I	N	G	L	Y	N	A	E	A	R
F	C	H	R	I	S	T	M	A	S	A	C	A	N	E
S	Y	A	D	H	T	R	I	B	O	M	E	C	D	K
N	U	F	L	I	P	G	L	O	S	S	L	H	B	O
S	H	O	P	P	I	N	G	R	K	Y	E	E	A	H
H	O	L	I	D	A	Y	S	M	A	O	T	S	G	C
N	E	E	N	I	H	S	N	U	S	B	S	K	S	B

- FRIENDS
- FUN
- GUM
- HANDBAGS
- HOLIDAYS
- HORSES
- ICE-CREAM
- JEANS
- LIPGLOSS
- MANICURES
- MOVIES
- PARTIES
- SHOPPING
- SLEEPOVERS
- SUNSETS
- SUNSHINE
- SURFING
- YOGA

- ACTING
- BOYS
- CANDLES
- DRIVING
- BEACHES
- BRACELETS
- CHOKERS
- FASHION
- BIRTHDAYS
- BROCCOLI
- CHRISTMAS
- FLIPFLOPS

Mary-Kate and Ashley have travelled all over the world to some really exciting places to make their videos and movies. Here are some of the countries and cities they've visited, plus lots more places. See how many you can find.

- ALABAMA
- AUSTRIA
- BELGIUM
- CALGARY
- CHICAGO
- CUBA
- FINLAND
- GERMANY
- GREECE
- HAWAII
- ICELAND
- ITALY
- LONDON
- LOS ANGELES
- MADRID
- MONTREAL
- NEW YORK
- NORWAY

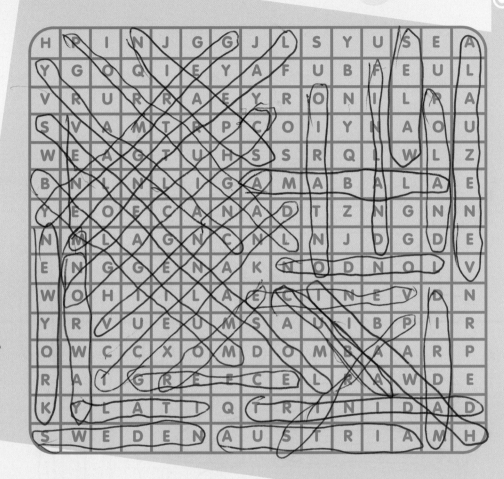

H	P	I	N	J	G	G	J	L	S	Y	U	S	E	A
Y	G	O	Q	I	E	Y	A	F	U	B	F	E	U	L
V	R	U	R	R	A	E	Y	R	O	N	I	L	P	A
S	V	A	M	T	P	P	C	O	I	Y	N	A	O	U
W	E	A	G	T	U	H	S	S	R	Q	L	W	L	Z
B	N	I	N	L	I	G	A	M	A	B	A	L	A	E
Y	E	O	F	C	A	N	A	D	T	Z	N	G	N	N
N	M	L	A	G	N	C	N	L	N	J	D	G	D	E
E	N	G	G	E	N	A	K	N	O	D	N	O	I	V
W	O	H	I	I	L	A	E	C	I	N	E	V	D	N
Y	R	V	U	E	U	M	S	A	U	I	B	P	I	R
O	W	C	C	X	O	M	D	O	M	B	A	A	R	P
R	A	I	G	R	E	E	C	E	L	P	A	W	D	E
K	Y	L	A	T	I	Q	T	R	I	N	I	D	A	D
S	W	E	D	E	N	A	U	S	T	R	I	A	M	H

- ONTARIO
- PARIS
- POLAND
- PORTUGAL
- ROME
- SPAIN
- SWEDEN
- TRINIDAD
- VENEZUALA
- VENICE
- VIENNA
- WALES

Did you find them all?
Well done!

Mary-Kate and Ashley

are already huge in Hollywood, but could you follow in
their footsteps to the Walk of Fame?
Find out if you've got what it takes by playing this board game.
First one to the Hollywood Hills is a winner!

Have you got what it takes to be a movie star?

41

42 You're interviewed by all the magazines. Move on 4 spaces

43

44

40 The press love the preview! Move on 3 spaces.

39

38

37 Rhearsals! Do a 2-minute dance routine or move back 3 spaces.

25

26

27 Sing the chorus of a song or move back 3 spaces.

28

24

23 You're late for rehearsal. Move back 3 spaces.

22

21 You give a great performance. Move on 3 spaces.

9 The director loves you, darling! Move on 3 spaces.

10

11 Oh, no! A rival steals your script. Move back 3 spaces.

12

8

7 You stop for a manicure. Lose a turn.

6

5 Your big chance! Sing a verse of your favourite hit or go back to the start.

How to play

You'll need a dice...

... some counters (buttons are good)

... and at least one friend!

45 Stop to sign autographs for fans. Miss a turn.

46

47 You get stage fright! Move back 6 spaces.

48

Hurrah! You've made it to Hollywood and you're in the movies!

HOLLYWOOD!

36

35 Great news – you've got the lead part in a fab movie! Move on 3 spaces.

34

33

29 You get a crush on your co-star! Float on 3 spaces.

30

31 You tear your gown in a big scene. Miss a turn for repairs.

32

20

19 You have to play a clown! Miss a turn while you sit in make-up.

18

17

13

14

15 You get the part! Move on two spaces.

16

4

3 You've got an audition! Move on 3 spaces.

2

1

START

Throw the dice. The player with the highest score goes first.

Roll the dice, and highest score starts

Follow any instructions on the squares you land on

First one to reach Hollywood wins!

Now You See Him, Now You Don't

continued from page 49

"He was really excited," Ashley replied. "He said no one has asked him to be part of the magic show in twenty years."

"And he doesn't mind that you're going to use his tie?" Mary-Kate asked.

"Well," Ashley hesitated. "I didn't exactly mention that part. You know how he is about his tie. He's always patting it, and he kind of moves away if you get too close to it – like he's protecting it or something. But his tie won't be damaged in my trick. I'm sure it will be fine."

"Here he is," Sean said as he led a grey horse to the exercise ring. "You asked for Sugar, you got Sugar. Good luck."

"Thanks, Sean." Mary-Kate took Sugar's reins.

"I hope Sugar's in a better mood than he was last time," Ashley said.

"Me, too," Mary-Kate agreed. She explained to Ashley how the trick worked.

"We need to get Sugar to shake his head," she said. "Horses naturally shake their heads when a fly bites them. It's like a reflex. If a fly bites a horse on the neck, he shakes his head no. If the horse is bitten on the chest, he nods his head yes."

"What does that have to do with the trick?" Ashley asked.

"When you hold up a card in your right hand, I'll scratch Sugar's neck and he'll shake his head no. When you hold up a card in your left hand, I'll scratch his chest and he'll nod his head yes."

"Cool," Ashley said. "So the scratch will act like the bug bite."

"Exactly," Mary-Kate replied. "After a while, just the sight of the card in someone's right hand or left hand should make him shake his head no or yes."

"Scratching him won't make him mad, will it?" Ashley asked, backing up.

"Nope," Mary-Kate replied. "So when I tell you to hold up a card, hold a card in front of him so he can see it. We'll do the right hand first, okay?"

Ashley glanced at the first card in the deck – a queen of hearts. "He doesn't charge when he sees red, does he?"

"Ashley, that's a bull, not a horse," Mary-Kate said. "Don't worry. Elliot will take over when he gets here."

Elliot had promised to come to the stables to rehearse the trick as soon as his wrestling practice was over. But Mary-Kate wanted to get a head start on training Sugar before he got there.

"Ready?" Mary-Kate held Sugar by the reins and stood on his left side. "Hold a card up in your right hand."

Ashley held up a card and said, "Is this your card?"

Mary-Kate scratched Sugar's neck. Sugar flicked his tail.

"That's weird," Mary-Kate said. "Every other horse I've known would shake his head. Let's try it again."

Ashley waved a card in her right hand. "Is this your card?" Mary-Kate scratched Sugar's neck again, a little harder this time.

Sugar snorted and reared up. "Stampede!" Ashley screamed.

Mary-Kate tightened her grip on Sugar's reins and calmed him down. "Don't panic," she told Ashley. "I must have scratched him a little too hard that time, that's all."

"Why don't you try teaching him yes?" Ashley suggested.

"Maybe that will be easier," Mary-Kate agreed. "Hold a card up in your left hand this time."

Ashley held up the card and repeated the question. Mary-Kate gingerly scratched Sugar on the chest. The horse bowed his head and butted Mary-Kate's hand with his nose.

Mary-Kate sighed with frustration. "I don't get it. Why is Sugar having so much trouble with this?" Mary-Kate had always trusted her instincts with horses – and they'd usually been right. She'd never misjudged one so badly before.

"Here I am!" Elliot walked into the exercise ring. "Is this the wonder horse? How's it going?"

"Um, okay," Mary-Kate said. "We just started training him."

"Let's see what you've got so far," Elliot said. Ashley handed the deck of cards to him. He held one up in his right hand. "Is this your card?" he asked Sugar.

Mary-Kate scratched Sugar on the neck. Sugar bucked slightly and spat at Elliot. The horse spit landed in his hair.

"Hey!" Elliot cried. "What's he doing?"

Ashley burst out laughing. But Mary-Kate was too worried to find it funny.

"We need a little more practice," she told him.

"Are you sure you know what you're doing?" Elliot asked.

Ashley rushed to her sister's defence. "Hey – if there's one thing Mary-Kate is an expert on, it's horses. She'll work it out."

"It had better work out," Elliot said, "because everybody in school is already buzzing about what a great act we have. But if this horse doesn't hurry up and learn this trick, we won't have an act!"

Mary-Kate didn't want to let everybody down. *Oh, Sugar*, she thought. *Was I wrong about you*?

"Give me some time alone with him," Mary-Kate said. "Maybe he'll be more obedient if he gets to know me better."

"All right, Mary-Kate," Elliot said. "But remember – the show is only two days away!"

Elliot and Ashley left. Mary-Kate struggled with Sugar. She tried everything she could think of. She spent the whole afternoon with him, but he made no progress. It was beginning to get dark when she finally decided to give up.

"It's hopeless." She sighed. She took the reins and led Sugar back into the barn.

Sean was cleaning out the next stall. He stopped sweeping when he saw her come in. "How did it go?" he asked.

"Terribly," Mary-Kate admitted. "I hate to say it, but I don't think I can train this horse. I'm going to have to tell Elliot I can't do the trick."

Sean looked sympathetic. "I still don't understand why you picked Sugar to train," he said. "He never listens to anything anyone says."

"That's not true," Mary-Kate insisted. "The first time I rode him he did everything I wanted him to do. He was the perfect horse."

"Sounds like you're talking about my Sugar!" a girl's voice called out.

Mary-Kate turned around. She saw a girl dressed in grey stretch jeans and a white sweater. Her long blonde hair was held back with a black velvet headband.

"That's Darcy Boyd," Sean explained. "She goes to Maplewood Academy."

Maplewood Academy was another nearby school. Mary-Kate's softball team played against Maplewood sometimes.

"You have a horse named Sugar, too?" Mary-Kate asked.

Darcy nodded. "We keep him in our own stable behind our house."

"Have you ever kept your horse here?" Mary-Kate asked.

Darcy nodded. "A few weeks ago my parents and I went on vacation," she explained. "So we kept Sugar here."

She stared at the horse Mary-Kate had brought in. "Actually, my Sugar is grey, too – in fact he looks an awful lot like that horse."

Sean smacked his forehead with his

palm.

"Oh, man! Why didn't it click?" he said. "You rode the day J.D. was here, when I was gone. He probably put you on Darcy's horse so he'd get some exercise."

Mary-Kate stared at Sean. "I can't believe it," she cried. "This whole time I've been trying to train the wrong horse!"

CHAPTER SEVEN

"Sorry, Mary-Kate," Sean said. "I should have figured out that you were talking about a different horse. But when you asked for Sugar, I just assumed you meant our Sugar!"

"It's amazing how much this Sugar looks like my Sugar," Darcy commented. "Except for the marks on their ankles."

"What do you mean?" Mary-Kate asked.

"This Sugar has a white patch on his right ankle," Darcy pointed out. "My Sugar doesn't. Other than that, they're practically identical."

"Darcy, can I ask you a big favour?" Mary-Kate crossed her fingers behind her back. "Do you think I could train your horse to be in the magic show at Harrington?"

Darcy's eyes lit up. "I went to that show last year," she said. "It was great!"

Mary-Kate told Darcy about Elliot's card trick. She explained that she wanted to train the horse to shake his head yes or no.

"What a neat trick!" Darcy said.

"So can Sugar be in the show with me?" Mary-Kate asked.

"I don't know," Darcy said, shaking her head. "Nobody ever trains Sugar but me."

"But think about it," Mary-Kate prodded. "Everyone will talk about how smart your horse is for months to come!"

Darcy grinned. "Okay. This could be fun. We can train him together."

"Great!" Mary-Kate sighed with relief.

"It shouldn't be hard to teach Sugar the trick. I teach him little tricks all the time," Darcy said.

"Terrific!" Mary-Kate said. "Thanks a million."

Darcy gave Mary-Kate her address. Mary-Kate would have to go to the Boyds' stable to work with the horse.

Mary-Kate said good-bye to Darcy and Sean. Then she climbed on to the shuttle bus back to school.

Thank goodness, Mary-Kate thought, dropping into a seat. *Darcy saved our magic trick!*

Now all I have to do is figure out a way to train a horse – in two days!

Ashley hurried to the Harrington auditorium. She'd been practising her tie-cutting trick all morning and was getting really good at it.

She found Ross on stage with Jeremy. They were pushing Ross's box to the middle of the stage.

"There you are!" Ross said.

"Ross just told me he had to rescue you from this box," Jeremy said. He grabbed his chest and fluttered his eyelashes. "My hero!"

Ashley frowned at her cousin. "You'd better watch it," she said. "Or you're going to be locked in there next."

"Ooh, I'm shaking," Jeremy said.

"Ready to practice, Ashley?" Ross interrupted.

"Before we start, I want to show you the tie trick I told you about," Ashley said. "I've got it down pretty well. Wait till you see it." Ross nodded as she took the loud colourful tie out of her pocket.

"Whoa!" Jeremy yelled when he saw the tie. "You stole Mr. Barber's tie."

"No, I didn't," Ashley said. "It just looks like Mr. Barber's tie."

She set the tie aside and pulled out two matching red ribbons. "Pretend this is Mr. Barber's tie," she said. Then she showed them the trick. First she took a top hat with two secret pockets – one on the left and one on the right – and placed it on the table. Then she cut one of the ribbons in half and stuffed it into the left pocket inside the top hat. She covered the hat with a scarf, said "Abracadabra," and showed the empty hat to the boys. Then she waved her hands over the hat and pulled out a red ribbon from the right pocket – whole and uncut.

Jeremy clapped. "Excellent!" Ross shouted. "That trick is going to bring down the house."

Ashley bowed. "Thank you, thank you."

"It's your trick, Ashley," Ross said. "You'll be the magician for it – and I'll be your assistant."

To be continued ... go to page 68

Mary-Kate and Ashley's
guide to shopping

Mary-Kate and Ashley just love to shop! But shopping isn't for wimps so here are a few hints'n'tips on how to shop till you drop.

What's your shopping style?

With a spare fiver you'd buy
a anything so long as it glitters
b a chunky choker
c magazines and sweets

Shopping secret
You can find some great bargains in charity shops!

You like shopping in
a funky fashion shops
b vintage or charity shops
c anywhere you can get good trainers and trackies

Your favourite outfit is
a a funky T-shirt and cropped jeans
b a long skirt and draped top
c vest top and tracksuit bottoms

Your idea of fun is
a a party where you can dress to impress
b a night in with a few girlfriends doing makeovers
c ordering a pizza and renting a movie

Mostly *a*'s
It doesn't matter what the latest is, you've just gotta have it! You have your finger on the fashion pulse and always know what rocks and what flops. You probably spend lots of time shopping, so read all the tips to make the most of your mall!

Mostly *b*'s
You like fashion, but you're a thoughtful type and you have your own ideas on what you like and what you don't. You prefer a vintage, retro look and take your time shopping around to find something special.

Mostly *c*'s
You love to have fun with your mates, and if that means shopping, fine, but you're just as happy reading your fave mags or playing sports out of doors. You like window-shopping, but don't feel disappointed if you don't buy anything.

Top shopping tips

* Decide how much you can afford to spend and don't go over it!

* Find a friend you can trust to go with you.

* Go to a mall or shopping centre where you have lots of choices.

* Wear comfy shoes!

* Schedule some pit-stops for lunch and breaks – you need to keep your strength up!

* Buy things you know you'll wear lots.

* Make sure the shop will let you bring things back if you change your mind.

Shopping secret

It's not about being a fashion victim, it's about having your own style!

THREE SHOPPING DON'TS

DON'T buy something that's too big or too small – make sure it's the right size for you now!

DON'T blow your budget on the first thing you see – shop around, you might see something better.

DON'T buy anything just because it's the latest thing – make sure it looks good on you!

THREE SHOPPING DOS

DO try everything on before you buy.

DO ask your friend for her honest opinion – that's why you brought her!

DO make sure whatever you buy goes with at least one thing you already have.

You know you're shopped out when...

You find you're looking for the size label on hair bobbles.

You come out of the changing room and your mate points out you're wearing the funky T-shirt back to front.

You wonder why you can't find your size, then realise you're looking at boys' clothes.

You think neon pink and lime green look strangely attractive together.

Shopping secret

You needn't spend a fortune to look cool – just a few new accessories can work wonders!

Your number's up

According to numerology – the study of numbers – you can tell a lot about yourself by finding your personal number. Here's one way to work it out! Write down your full name. Then, using the grid below, find out which number goes with which letter and add them all together, like this, until you reach a single number:

M	A	R	Y	-	K	A	T	E		O	L	S	E	N
4 +	1 +	9 +	7 +	2 +	1 +	2 +	5 +			6 +	3 +	1 +	5 +	5	= 51 5 + 1 = 6

So Mary-Kate's number is 6...

A	S	H	L	E	Y		F	U	L	L	E	R
1 +	1 +	8 +	3 +	5 +	7 +		6 +	3 +	3 +	3 +	5 +	9 +

O	L	S	E	N
6 +	3 +	1 +	5 +	5	= 74 7 + 4 = 11 1 + 1 = 2

... and Ashley's number is 2!

Now check out *your* lucky number.

1	2	3	4	5	6	7	8	9
A	B	C	D	E	F	G	H	I
J	K	L	M	N	O	P	Q	R
S	T	U	V	W	X	Y	Z	

LOUISE   MORGAN
3+6+3+9+1+5 + 4 +6+9+7+1+5 = 59 = 5+9 = 14 = 1+4 = 5
9 12 21 22 27   31   37 46 53 54 59

62

1 You're a live wire and love to try new things. You love a challenge, too, and have a strong streak of willpower that means you're bound to succeed! You have your own quirky way of dressing and expressing yourself, and you aren't afraid to take the lead. You can occasionally be a bit bossy.

Love: your own way, kooky clothes, sports
Hate: being held back, being broke, being bossed around

2 You're gentle and sensitive and you're happy to share your stuff with your mates. You're good at sorting out what's really important from what's just small stuff, and you're able to calm your pals down when they're having a major trauma. Sometimes you can be a bit *too* sensitive – just don't let it get to you!

Love: music, being on your own, helping people
Hate: ear-splitting songs, tough decisions, arguments

3 You're confident and outgoing, and love meeting people. You'd rather be out and about than stuck indoors. You're bright, sparky and fun to be with, and take problems in your stride. You adapt well to new situations and are popular with your friends, but take care that, in your rush, you don't leave a trail of chaos behind.

Love: outdoor sports, anything mystical, hanging out with friends
Hate: criticism, being cooped up, dull routines

4 You love woods, mountains and feeling close to nature, although indoors you like to be warm and cosy. You're responsible and hard working, and your friends find you very 'grounding' to talk to. You're capable and determined so, when you want something, you usually succeed in getting it.

Love: shopping, cooking, feeling in control
Hate: monotony, cold weather, laziness

5 You are *seriously* adventurous, and thrive on excitement and challenges. You're inquisitive, love change and often try new things. You're happy to change your plans at a moment's notice because you like to be spontaneous. A natural communicator, you're popular with your friends, who love the way you're always up for it!

Love: chocolate, most kinds of sport, languages
Hate: being in a rut, being alone, silence

6 You love beautiful things, whether it's clothes, make-up or jewellery, and your room is a total girlfest when it comes to decoration. You enjoy being at home, and love having sleepovers and parties with your mates at your place. You're a good listener when your friends need to moan, and your strong sense of justice means you can hand out good advice.

Love: looking good, food, romance
Hate: being taken for granted, intolerance, mess

7 You're so sensitive, your mates sometimes wonder if you can read their minds! You're a bit of a dreamer, and your imagination often swings into overdrive, but at the same time you can be practical and organised. You can be a bit of a perfectionist, but make sure you're not so picky that nothing's good enough for you!

Love: mystery, daydreaming, clothes
Hate: crowds, pollution, dishonesty

8 You have bags of energy, and you love to succeed and be the best. At school you aren't afraid of hard work, and you're a brilliant organiser whenever there's an event on. You like clothes, CDs and DVDs, jewellery and – of course – shoes! You have loads of charm, but sometimes you can be a bit too serious – don't forget to lighten up!

Love: having loads of money, making lists, being in charge
Hate: bullies, grouches, being told what to do

9 You're warm, open and friendly, and get on really well with other people. You often rely on your instinct to tell you what to do, and you're usually right. You're happy to go with the flow when you and your mates are deciding what to do and where to go, but you have very firm opinions on what's right and wrong and won't be swayed.

Love: swimming, pampering yourself, relaxing
Hate: selfishness, injustice, being pressured

Mary-Kate and Ashley's
guide to great hair

Bad hair days – who needs 'em! Follow this guide to great hair and you can say goodbye to hair horror days and hello to hair-hair-hair hooray! days. Find out the best look for you and how to deal with seriously scary hair problems.

Check out the statements below and tick those that apply to you. Then check what colour you've picked most of to see what kind of hair you have.

☆ My hair is usually shiny.

☆ On a bad hair day, my hair looks like straw.

☆ I need to wash my hair two or three times a week.

☆ My hair looks like it's been rained on a couple of days after I've washed it.

Mostly green
You've got the greasies! It can be annoying having hair that looks as though it needs to be washed when you've just done it, but don't worry, there are loads of things you can do to help that don't involve wearing a hat all the time to cover up! Read on for some great tips.

☆ My hair-grips and bobbles sometimes slide out.

☆ My hair sometimes gets really frizzy and tangled.

☆ I can usually run a comb through without meeting any knots.

☆ I sometimes get (eek!) dandruff.

Mostly yellow
Your hair is on the dry side, and needs lots of tender loving care to make sure it looks its best. Make sure you don't over-use hairdryers, and leave your hair to dry naturally as often as you can.

☆ I need to wash my hair every couple of days or it looks lank.

☆ I have split ends.

☆ On a bad hair day, my hair looks like string.

Mostly pink
Lucky you! You have normal hair, and you don't need too much work to keep it looking good. Make sure you follow all our hints and tips to keep your hair in good shape.

☆ I can wear my hair loose or tied back and it feels fine both ways.

Hair-raising fact

We lose around **50 – 100** hairs every day.

Three hair dos...

✓ Do use a wide-toothed comb on damp hair to gently untangle any knots, otherwise it's Ouch!

✓ Do get your hair trimmed regularly – it's the only way to deal with those nasty old split ends!

✓ Do be gentle when you're removing hair bobbles and bands – you want hair care, not hair tear!

Top tips for great hair

Your body needs vitamins and minerals to grow great hair, so eat your fruits and veggies every day!

Once or twice a week, gently massage your scalp for a few minutes to stimulate the circulation to your head.

Always wash your hair after you've been swimming, at the beach or the pool – salt and chlorine are real shine-stealers!

When you're blow drying, use the coolest setting possible to avoid frazzled hair.

Always wear a hat if you're in the sun – your hair can burn just like the rest of you!

Avoid sharing hairbrushes, combs and accessories with friends – you love your mates, but some things are too personal to share!

Exercise is important for your hair, believe it or not – it stimulates the circulation, which is good for your follicles!

Wrap a towel around wet hair and press gently, rather than rubbing dry – much kinder to your hair!

Hair-raising fact

It takes anything from **2 to 6 years** for a hair to grow from your scalp **to the end**.

Hair-raising fact

Hair grows around **half-an-inch** a month – and it's faster in the summer!

... and three hair don'ts

✗ Don't use plain rubber bands on your hair – you'll tear your poor old tresses to pieces!

✗ Don't brush your hair when it's wet, as this is when it's most prone to damage.

✗ Don't pull your hair back into a pony-tail so tight it makes your eyes water, as this can weaken your hair.

Mary-Kate and Ashley's
guide to the stars

Mary-Kate and Ashley have their birthday on 13 June. This means that their star sign is – yes, you've probably guessed it – Gemini, the sign of the twins. Geminis are charming, entertaining, have lots of interests, and make great friends. Sounds just like Mary-Kate and Ashley! How typical are you of your star sign? Read on and find out…

Aries
21 March – 19 April

Aries girls love a challenge. You play to win, and you can really inspire your friends. You like to be active, and you're more likely to be out with your mates than vegging out on the sofa. You're always up for adventure, and you're great at putting on a brave face when the going gets tough !

Taurus
20 April – 20 May

You're usually calm and easy-going, but when you do decide to have a tantrum, you have everyone running for cover! You like music and you have an arty side, and at school you find that, once you've learned something, you don't forget it easily.

Leo
23 July – 22 August

Leos love excitement, so you're usually at the centre of attention! You're popular, affectionate and generous, and like being the leader. You may have been a bit of a tomboy when you were younger, but nowadays you always make sure you look good and you know how to turn on the charm.

Gemini
21 May – 20 June

Geminis just love to be on the go. You're a real gadget girl and feel lost without your mobile phone! You're able to look on the bright side even when things are gloomy, and you're good at noticing little details. You're sometimes able to tell how people are feeling even when they don't say anything.

Cancer
21 June – 22 July

Cancerians are home bunnies. You're happy with your own company, but your friends love having you around, and you always come through for them when they're in trouble. You're close to your emotions, and enjoy creative hobbies such as painting, writing, music or acting.

Virgo
23 August – 22 September

You're practical, orderly and efficient, and a great organiser – you're usually on top of your homework and get things done on time. You're quick to learn new things, and like to be busy. You can be witty and charming, but you're happiest with a small circle of really close friends rather than with big crowds.

Libra
23 September – 22 October

You may seem all sweetness and light on the surface, but underneath you're a feisty go-getter! A bit of a style queen, you love clothes and take your time deciding what to wear. Your friends know they can rely on you to keep a secret, because although you love to chat, you don't gossip.

Scorpio
23 October – 21 November

You know what you want and you're all set to get it! You choose friends carefully, and they like you because they know they can rely on you for good advice. You go your own way rather than following others, and sometimes you need to get away from it all to recharge.

Sagittarius
22 November – 21 December

You often find you're doing several things at once because you have so much energy. You can be a bit of a rebel, but you understand that most rules are there for a reason. Your friends are probably a pretty mixed bunch and you hate to be stuck in a groove, so get busy.

Aquarius
20 January – 18 February

You're great at coming up with unusual ideas, and you may not dress like everyone else, but you always look stunning. You have lots of friends, but they never know what you're going to do next – Aquarius girls are never predictable!

Capricorn
22 December – 19 January

With your unflappable nature, you're great to have around in a crisis because you won't panic – you'll just deal, calmly and quietly. At school you work hard and you're good at organising your work schedule, but you know when to take time out. When it comes to fashion, you're no victim – you choose your own style.

Pisces
19 February – 20 March

Pisces girls have amazing imaginations and you love daydreaming and making up stories. You're very creative, and you're drawn to all things mystical and magical! Your friends like you because you're so good at understanding their problems. You're emotional, intuitive and sensitive.

Now You See Him, Now You Don't

continued from page 59

"Great!" Ashley said. Now they were more of a team than ever.

"But, Ashley, you're not going to cut Mr. Barber's tie in half, are you?" Jeremy asked.

Ashley explained that she was going to pretend to cut Mr. Barber's tie in half. But she would really be cutting the fake tie.

"You'd better not mess up that trick," Jeremy warned. "Barber freaks out if anyone even touches his tie."

"I know," Ashley said. "That's what makes the trick extra-funny."

"Once a student bumped into his tie with a chocolate ice cream bar," Jeremy went on. "Barber was so upset, he cancelled class for the day so he could go to the dry cleaner."

"You made that story up," Ashley said. "Didn't you, Jeremy?"

"Okay, so I did," Jeremy admitted. "But I'd be extra careful if I were you."

"You're not going to get us in trouble," Ross asked. "Are you, Ashley?"

"Of course not," Ashley insisted. "This trick is a piece of cake. Nothing can possibly go wrong."

She flashed him a nervous grin. *At least, I hope nothing will go wrong*, she thought. *Or Mr. Barber will never forgive me – and neither will Ross!*

CHAPTER EIGHT

"Okay, Sugar." Darcy Boyd stood in front of her horse and held up a card in her right hand. "Is this your card?"

Mary-Kate was standing outside the Boyds' stable, holding Sugar – the good Sugar – by his reins. She gently scratched him on the neck. Sugar shook his head no.

"Good boy!" Mary-Kate cried. She fed him a carrot to reward him.

Darcy patted his nose. Mary-Kate rubbed the smooth grey hair on his neck. It really was amazing how much Darcy's horse looked like the other Sugar. But their personalities couldn't be more different.

Darcy and Mary-Kate practised the trick with Sugar over and over again. Before long Sugar shook his head no without being scratched. All he needed was to see the card in Darcy's right hand and hear her ask the question.

"You're so lucky, Darcy," Mary-Kate said. "Sugar is a great horse."

"Isn't he?" Darcy agreed. "But you're really good with him, too, Mary-Kate. I can tell you know what you're doing – and so can Sugar."

Mary-Kate gave Sugar another piece of carrot.

"I think it's so cool we're teaching him this trick," Darcy added. "Sugar loves attention!"

"He'll get plenty of it at the magic

show," Mary-Kate said. "Now let's teach him to say yes."

Sugar quickly learned to nod yes when Mary-Kate touched his chest. *This is really working!* Mary-Kate thought. She could feel her excitement growing.

This trick really is going to steal the show!

"Why did I ever agree to be your stand-in?" Ashley asked. She and Mary-Kate were on their way to the Harrington auditorium for the magic show dress rehearsal.

"Because you're my sister and you love me," Mary-Kate said. "And I promised you could borrow my brand-new sweater," she added.

Mary-Kate and Ashley walked into the auditorium and tossed their coats onto one of the seats. Mary-Kate scanned the room, looking for Elliot. About twenty people were there, waiting their turn to rehearse on stage.

"Hey, Mary-Kate." Elliot waved from the back row. "Over here."

Mary-Kate and Ashley walked up the aisle to join him.

"What's she doing here?" Elliot asked, eyeing Ashley suspiciously. "She's part of the competition."

"It's not a competition, Elliot," Mary-Kate said. "And I asked Ashley to stand in for Sugar."

"But how's the real horse doing?" Elliot asked. "Did you teach him the trick?"

"It's been going great," Mary-Kate told him. "Once Sugar nodded his head yes when I gave the signal for no, but every other time he was perfect."

"Okay," Elliot said. "But he'd better not mess up at the show. Everyone will be paying extra-close attention to us. I made sure that we're the grand finale!"

Elliot, Mary-Kate, and Ashley went up on to the stage. Jeremy was at a microphone, acting as the emcee. He was wearing his black cape and top hat.

"And now, ladies and gentlemen, let's give a huge hand to the one and only Elliot Weber!" Jeremy said.

Elliot walked out on to the stage wearing a wireless microphone clipped to his T-shirt.

"Thank you, thank you," he said, bowing. "Ladies and gentlemen, tonight I am going to perform an amazing feat of mind-reading using only a deck of cards. But first, allow me to introduce my partner, Mary-Kate Burke, and Sugar the Wonder Horse!"

That was Mary-Kate's cue. She hurried onto the stage, leading Ashley by a string tied around her wrist.

The kids watching from the audience all broke out laughing. Some of them whistled and hooted.

Ashley turned bright red. "You owe me big time for this one!" she whispered to Mary-Kate.

"And now," Elliot went on, "I am going to ask my brilliant partner to pick a card from this brand-new deck."

Elliot went on with the trick. First he blindfolded himself. Then he spread out the cards and let Mary-Kate choose one. She held it up for Ashley and the audience to see.

After showing the card to the audience, Mary-Kate put it back in the deck.

Elliot went on, running through the whole trick. He held up various cards to Ashley.

"Sugar the Wonder Horse, is this Mary-Kate's card?" Elliot asked.

Ashley shook her head no.

Then he picked another card. "Is this it?"

Ashley shook her head no again.

"Good girl," Mary-Kate said, feeding Ashley a lump of sugar.

Everyone in the audience laughed harder.

"Hey!" Mary-Kate giggled as Ashley spit the sugar cube in her direction. But she could see that Ashley was laughing, too.

Finally, after some more hocus-pocus, Elliot opened a sealed envelope. "Is this your card?" he asked Ashley.

Ashley nodded her head yes.

Elliot turned to the audience of other magicians. "What did you think?" he asked.

"Your horse is kind of funny-looking," someone called out from the seats. Everyone laughed.

"Yeah!" someone else said. "I hope it goes that well with the real horse."

Elliot looked hard at Mary-Kate. "So do I," he whispered.

"Don't worry," Mary-Kate replied. "I guarantee it will. Sugar won't let us down."

"What do you think?" Ashley asked Mary-Kate. "Too heavy on the sequins?"

Mary-Kate and Ashley were in Ashley's dorm room putting the finishing touches on their costumes.

Ashley twirled around to model the outfit she was wearing for the magic show that night – a pair of black tights and a long-sleeved black leotard. The arms and legs were decorated with colourful swirls of sequins.

Ashley had sewn a triple row of sequins around the ankles, since her feet were going to show more than anything else. Her hair was held back in a ponytail with a sequin-covered scrunchie.

"I like it," Mary-Kate said. "Besides, you always said there's no such thing as too many sequins."

"It's true," Ashley laughed. "Especially when it comes to magicians' costumes. Wait until you see the fake feet!" she added. "They have sequins around the ankles, too. They look just like the real things."

She glanced down at the rabbit cage on the floor. The door was open – and the rabbit was gone.

Ashley sighed. "The rabbit escaped from his cage again! He's always doing that!"

Mary-Kate helped her search the room. "How does he open the door?" she asked.

"I have no idea," Ashley replied. "He's got to be in here somewhere." She opened the wardrobe door.

Mary-Kate checked under the bed. "Here he is," she said, scooping the rabbit into her arms. "He was hiding behind the dust bunnies under your bed!"

"Ha-ha-ha." Ashley took the rabbit

and put him back in the cage. "Now stay in there!" she ordered. She set a trainer against the door to block it.

"Has Phoebe named him yet?" Mary-Kate asked.

Ashley shook her head. "She should name him Houdini," she said. "After that magician who was a famous escape artist."

"That's perfect!" Phoebe exclaimed as she slipped into the room. She hurried to the cage and wiggled her finger at the rabbit. "I've been trying to come up with a name for days. From now on we'll call him Houdini."

"Wow, Phoebe," Mary-Kate said. "You look awesome."

Phoebe was wearing a long satin skirt and the vintage fur-trimmed sweater. "I was trying to match the rabbit," Phoebe said, petting the white fur on her sweater.

"What are you going to do with Houdini once the show's over?" Mary-Kate asked. She knew Ashley didn't want the rabbit to stay in their room. He was cute, but they could get into trouble if Ms. Viola found him.

"Max's parents and little sister are coming to the show," Phoebe told her. "Max is going to let his sister keep Houdini." She sighed. "I'm going to miss him. But it's for the best."

"I have butterflies in my stomach," Mary-Kate confessed. "What if Sugar messes up Elliot's card trick?"

"What if I mess up in the magicians' box?" Ashley worried.

"None of us is going to mess up tonight," Phoebe said.

She looked at Mary-Kate's costume and smiled. Phoebe had lent her the vintage riding outfit: jodhpurs and black boots, and a lacy white silk blouse with ruffles on top.

"You look like a real horsewoman in that outfit," Phoebe said.

"Speaking of horses, how is Sugar getting to the show?" Ashley asked.

"Darcy called to say it's all set," Mary-Kate explained. "Sean is going to pick up Sugar at Darcy's stable and drive him to the show in his horse trailer."

"Sounds good!" Ashley said. She looked at her watch and gasped. "We'd better go. It's almost showtime."

There was a knock on the door. "Phoebe? Ashley?"

"It's Ms. Viola!" Phoebe whispered. She quickly shoved the rabbit cage behind the bed.

Phoebe nodded at Ashley, who called, "Come in."

Ms. Viola poked her head into the room. "Mary-Kate, there you are. You have a telephone call," she said. "It sounds important."

Who could it be? Mary-Kate wondered. "Thanks, Ms. Viola," she said.

"We'll meet you at the bus stop," Ashley said, putting on her jacket.

"Okay," Mary-Kate replied. She hurried out of the room to pick up the hall phone.

To be continued ... go to page 78

Mary-Kate and Ashley's
guide to holidays

Yay, it's the holidays! But how to make sure you don't get bored?
Read on for your best-ever guide on how to handle the holidays.

Your ideal summer day would be

a) Going swimming with your mates.
b) Lying on a beach sipping something cool.
c) Heading for a barbecue in your cutest sundress.

Holiday hint
Stay out of the sun between 12 and 3, when it's at its hottest.

What do you *really* feel when the summer holidays arrive?

a) Fantasic – what else?
b) You love summer, but you sometimes run out of ideas for things to do!
c) You have loads of things to do, and wish school never had to interrupt your social life.

Your folks have won the lottery and you can go anywhere you like for your holidays! You choose:

a) Something adventurous like skiing.
b) Disneyland!
c) A swanky hotel spa for lots of luxurious pampering.

Your folks haven't won the lottery and you're stuck in a caravan on a rainy day. Do you:

a) Put on your Wellies and a waterproof – nothing keeps you indoors.
b) Grab the games board and get ready for a day of winning.
c) Curl up with a magazine and catch up on celebrity gossip.

Holiday hint
Use a hair conditioner with added sunscreen for extra protection.

72

Holiday hint

Drink lots of water so you don't get dehydrated.

Keeping it cool

Always use a sun cream with a minimum of factor 15, and reapply every hour.

*

Stay fresh-faced – loads of make-up looks scary in bright sunlight!

*

If your face has gone red, a cool green-tinted moisturiser will help calm things down.

*

Stay stylish in the sun with funky sarongs, T-shirts and sun-hats.

*

Don't overdo fizzy drinks and ice-cream. Try sugar-free squash or mineral water and fruit juice.

Holiday romance – will it last?

You know it'll last when

♥ You think that might actually be a *tear* in his eye when you hug goodbye!

♥ He asks you for your address and phone number fourteen times before you leave.

♥ He's trying to persuade his folks to move to your home town.

You know it won't last when

❋ He somehow never gets around to giving you his phone number.

❋ He's more interested in burgers and barbecues than moonlit walks along the beach.

❋ He calls you Sarah. Your name isn't Sarah.

Mostly a's

Action girl! You love to be out and about and can't stand being cooped up indoors. You need adventure, so find some fun classes to go to – skating, indoor skiing or snorkelling could be fun.

Mostly b's

You're a beach babe! You like lots of things to do, so mix your days in the sun with trips to interesting places. Keep a stack of books and games at hand for when you can't go out and you'll never have a dull moment!

Mostly c's

Luxury lady! Holidays mean you can really indulge your passion for fashion. Make the most of escaping the school uniform and arrange sleepovers with your friends so you can swap style tips.

Looking for some new things to do on holiday? How about

Try a new food. Octopus? Snails? Well, maybe…

*

Try a new activity. Ever been skating? Rollerblading? Trampolining?

*

Read a book you'd normally never try. Love romances? Try a mystery.

*

Practise a brand new look. Normally sporty? For once, try flirty!

*

Learn to cook something! Chocolate cake? Pizza? Then invite some friends to help you eat it.

Mary-Kate and Ashley's
Word Searches

Here are two more fab wordsearches for you!
Words can go up, down, sideways or diagonally.

Mary-Kate and Ashley like broccoli and ice-cream, and loads of other stuff,
too. Hidden in the square below are lots of yummy nibbles, some healthy,
some special treats. See how many of them you can find.

- APPLE
- AUBERGINES
- BISCUIT
- BROCCOLI
- BURGERS
- CABBAGE
- CAKE
- CARROTS
- CHEESE
- CHERRIES
- CHIPS
- CHOCOLATE
- CRISPS
- CRUMPETS
- FISH
- HAM
- ICE CREAM
- KIWI FRUIT

- LETTUCE
- MELON
- MERINGUES

- MILKSHAKES
- NOODLES
- NOUGAT

- PIZZA
- ROAST CHICKEN
- SAUSAGES

- SCONES
- SPAGHETTI
- TOMATOES

Hidden in the square below are thirty boys' and girls' names. All of them feature in Mary-Kate and Ashley's books or vidoes. See how many you can spot!

- ALEX
- AMANDA
- AMBER
- ASHLEY
- CAMPBELL
- CHERYL
- CHLOE
- DANA
- DEVON
- ELISE
- JAKE
- JANE
- JEREMY
- JORDAN
- KRISTIN
- LARRY
- MANUELO
- MARY-KATE

M	Q	F	R	I	S	H	C	Z	V	J	T	C	E	P
P	A	O	A	E	D	A	O	L	E	U	N	A	M	P
A	S	R	R	Z	M	E	E	J	O	R	D	A	N	E
S	D	E	Y	P	E	D	T	E	E	N	H	O	C	C
W	M	N	B	K	K	N	A	M	B	G	S	L	P	D
Y	V	E	A	E	A	I	M	I	Y	E	H	I	E	E
U	L	H	L	M	U	T	B	C	D	C	L	V	L	Y
L	A	M	Y	R	A	S	E	H	N	H	O	A	E	E
T	D	N	R	O	N	I	R	E	E	N	R	L	V	P
S	Z	B	E	X	A	R	O	L	W	D	H	P	Q	I
M	U	X	H	Y	P	K	X	L	U	S	Z	H	E	Z
K	I	M	C	A	N	A	D	E	A	A	B	O	X	W
K	C	S	M	R	I	L	E	Y	A	R	R	E	I	S
O	E	J	T	E	Y	R	R	A	L	T	L	B	D	A
P	E	R	R	Y	R	F	G	S	H	A	Q	E	P	D

- MICHELLE
- MISTY
- PERRY

- PHOEBE
- RILEY
- ROSS

- ROXY
- SIERRA
- SUMMER

- TEDI
- VALERIE
- WENDY

Did you find them all?
Well done!

Mary-Kate and Ashley's
guide to colour

Mary-Kate likes maroon and Ashley loves yellow, but did you know that colours can reveal your personality? Find out your style with this fun quiz. Read each statement below and tick each one you agree with. Then check out your result.

I often suggest what my friends and I should do next.

I'll try anything once, but won't do it again if it's not fun.

I like being out of doors.

Mostly reds

You're a real action girl, and you put loads of energy into everything you do, whether it's stormtrooping the mall with your mates, or giving them what for on the sports field. You could try slowing down once in a while – a night off won't hurt you!

I hate sitting still for too long!

I don't plan too far ahead – I like to be spontaneous!

I like doing projects in pairs rather than working in a group.

Mostly greens

You love peace and harmony, and you're not the type to make a fuss, but if things aren't going your way you'll make sure they change until you're happy. You make a good friend because you hate bullying and stand up for other people.

I usually go with the flow rather than making a fuss.

I like nature – sunsets, seashores and woodlands rock!

I love action movies best.

Funky colours to suit your mood

Feeling funky? Want to party? Or are you more laid-back?
Whatever you feel, here are the colours you need to boost your mood.

You feel	You need
Energetic – you're dying to get up and go!	Red – on your trainers, T-shirt or party dress, guaranteed to fire you up!
Inspired – today you feel like writing a story or doing a fab painting.	Blue – have this colour in sight to boost your brain power and creativity.
Dreamy – you want to let nature flow over you.	Green – if you can't get out to hug a tree, try some leafy green plants in your room.
Fun – you want to hang out with your mates and have a laugh.	Yellow – to boost friendly feelings, wear a yellow top or hair accessories.
Cosy – you want to chill out on the sofa with a pile of DVDs.	Pink – snuggle up under a pink pashmina or wrap for your best chill-out ever.
Hard-working – you're going to tackle that pile of homework!	Brown – this will make you feel strong and positive (not sure chocolate counts, though!).

I'm usually the first among my friends to try a new look.

I love calm, peaceful days.

I love trying the latest fashions.

Mostly blues

You're the natural type. You love looking at nature, and have an air of calm and peace about you that your friends really love. You're good at expressing how you feel and tuning in to other people's moods.

Mostly purples

The words 'zany' and 'crazy' could have been invented for you! You're quick-witted, fun to be with and love thinking up new things to do so you and your mates don't get bored. You like working in groups – all the more people to have fun with!

COLOUR MATCHES

- Lime and deep purple – honestly, it works!
- Black and – just about anything! But don't go head-to-toe unless you want the vampire look.
- Cream and chocolate brown – you'll look good enough to eat!
- Yellow and blue – for a real sunshine look.
- Gold and russet – a great warming combo.

COLOUR CLASHES

- Pink and red – don't go there.
- Brown and black – they drain each other's energy.
- Orange and purple – they fight too hard together.
- Lime and lilac – that moment is so over.
- Grey and navy – unless you want to look like you're wearing a uniform.

continued from page 71

TWO of a kind

"Hello?" she said into the receiver.

"Mary-Kate?" a voice said. "It's Sean."

"Sean!" Mary-Kate said happily. "How's Sugar doing? Is he ready for his big debut?"

"That's why I'm calling," Sean said. "I have basketball practice at school tonight. So I asked J.D. to bring Sugar to the show. Is that okay?"

"Fine with me," Mary-Kate told Sean. "As long as someone brings him."

"Cool," Sean said. "Break a leg tonight. But not Sugar's."

Mary-Kate laughed. "Thanks." She hung up and hurried to catch up with Phoebe and Ashley at the shuttle bus.

When the girls reached the auditorium, the place was buzzing with excitement. Girls from White Oak were hanging out in the aisles, talking to the Harrington guys. There were lots of people Mary-Kate didn't recognise, many of them from the neighbouring towns. Most of the Harrington and White Oak faculty had turned out for the show, too. Mary-Kate saw her roommate, Campbell, and their friends Elise Van Hook and Samantha Kramer sitting in the third row. They smiled and gave the girls thumbs-up signs.

"We can't wait to see your acts!" Campbell cheered.

Phoebe and Ashley waved. "I have to go find my horse," Mary-Kate called. "I'll see you later!"

Backstage, students dressed in glittery costumes were running around collecting props. Mary-Kate saw magic wands, rings, ropes, and birds. She opened the back door to see if Sugar was waiting for her in the yard behind the auditorium. There was no sign of a horse anywhere.

"Hey, Mary-Kate," Elliot said, walking up to her and peering out the door. "Where's the star of the show?"

"He should be here any minute," Mary-Kate said nervously.

"Great." Elliot smiled and walked away.

Mary-Kate walked over to Ross and Ashley. Ross was wearing black jeans, a crisp white shirt, and a black cape.

"I've got something for you," Ross was saying to Ashley. He reached into the pocket of his jeans and pulled out a small white box tied with a red ribbon. "Open it," he said.

"A present?" Ashley asked. "What for?"

Ross glanced down at his feet. "I still felt bad about our fight," he said. "I just wanted to get you something to show how glad I am that we're partners."

"Wow, Ross," Ashley said. "That's so sweet." She untied the ribbon and lifted the lid. A pair of pretty silver earrings with pink stones rested on a little square of cotton in the box.

"Oh, Ross, I love them!" Ashley threw her arms around his neck and gave him a hug.

"For good luck," he said. "Our tricks are going to be great tonight. Both of them."

Ashley smiled as she put on the earrings. They looked beautiful on her. Mary-Kate was really happy for her sister.

Too bad she was a nervous wreck!

Mary-Kate went to peek outside again when she heard Jeremy starting his emcee speech.

Oh, no! Mary-Kate thought. The show was about to begin and Sugar was nowhere in sight!

CHAPTER NINE

Ashley hopped up and down with nervous excitement as she watched the show from the wings. Phoebe and Max got a big round of applause for their rabbit trick. And Marty Silver came up with a great mind-reading trick that totally dazzled the audience.

"Ashley!" Mary-Kate whispered. "Hide me!" She ducked down behind her sister.

"Mary-Kate, what are you doing?" Ashley asked.

"I can't let Elliot find me," Mary-Kate said. "J.D. hasn't brought Sugar yet. I tried calling the stables, but no one answered. What if they don't show up?"

Ashley shook her head sympathetically. "I'll keep my fingers crossed. And I'll try to stall on my trick to give you more time."

From the stage, Jeremy was announcing the next act. "And now, Ross Lambert and his lovely partner, Ashley Burke!" he said.

"Ready?" Ross asked, coming up behind Ashley. Together, they pushed the box out onto the stage. Ashley beamed her brightest smile at the audience.

"Ladies and gentlemen," Ross said in a deep, serious voice. "I am going to need complete silence for the next few minutes, because the trick I am about to perform is extremely dangerous."

He kept talking while Ashley slipped into the box. When all the latches were locked, he twirled around the table. Now the audience couldn't see Ashley's feet, because they were facing the back of the stage.

Please let me switch the feet in time, Ashley silently prayed.

As fast as she could, she pulled her feet out of the holes and stuck the fake feet in. Then she pulled the lever and quickly lowered herself into the secret compartment.

I did it! Ashley thought. *That was my best time yet*!

Ross swung the table around and picked up the saw.

"This saw is so sharp," Ross said, "we have an ambulance standing by outside, just in case!"

Ashley turned to the audience and faked a look of fright.

Ross placed the saw in the slit in the middle of the box. He sawed back and

forth with huge sweeps.

"Ouch!" Ashley cried. She winked at Ross. The audience gasped.

"Not to worry," Ross said. "My partner won't feel a thing . . . after this!" He pulled the box apart in two pieces.

The crowd gasped even louder.

"Tada!" Ashley said. The audience cheered and clapped.

Then Ross swung the table around again. Ashley raised herself out of the secret compartment, switched the feet back, and hopped out of the box. The audience applauded again.

Ross smiled at Ashley. "You did a great job," he whispered.

"We make a great team," Ashley replied.

"Thank you," Ross said to the audience. "And now, Ashley is going to perform her famous tie-cutting trick and I'm going to assist her." Ross ran off the stage.

What's he doing? Ashley wondered. A second later, she watched as he ran back onstage wearing a sequined T-shirt – that matched her costume!

The audience burst out laughing. Ashley gasped in surprise and then started laughing, too. He'd kept the matching T-shirt a secret – just to surprise her!

"How did you manage to match my costume?" she whispered to him.

"I've got spies," he replied, nodding at Phoebe, who watched from the wings.

Ross grinned and wheeled a small table

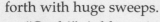

up to the microphone. On the table was a big top hat. Inside the hat were the two secret pockets. In the left pocket was the duplicate of Mr. Barber's tie.

"For this trick I need a volunteer from the audience," Ashley said. She looked out into the crowd. "Mr. Barber, would you like to help me, please?"

Mr. Barber smiled and made his way to the stage.

"I have a question for the audience," Ashley went on. "Would anyone like to see Mr. Barber's tie cut in half?"

The crowd went totally wild. Everyone yelled and cheered. "Yeah!" they screamed.

Everyone except Mr. Barber. "You didn't tell me this would have anything to do with my tie." He frowned.

"Trust me," Ashley said, winking at him. "Would you take off your tie, please?"

Mr. Barber shook his head. "Sorry," he went on. "But this tie is really special to me. Nothing can happen to it."

"Bar-ber, Bar-ber, Bar-ber!" the audience chanted.

"Please, Mr. Barber," Ashley begged. "I promise nothing will happen to your tie."

Mr. Barber hesitated. "Okay," he said. "But I hope you know what you're doing."

The teacher gave Ashley his tie and she walked over to the table with the hat.

"As you can see," Ashley said, "this top hat is empty."

She turned the hat upside down to prove it. Then she placed Mr. Barber's tie in the hat and covered the hat with a big silk scarf.

"Now, thanks to my magical powers, I

am able to create an energy field around the tie," Ashley said. "An energy field that will make it impossible to harm this tie, no matter what I do!"

She reached under the cloth and felt around inside the hat. Mr. Barber's tie was loosely draped inside. The duplicate tie was still tucked into the left pocket.

"Can you feel the energy?" Ashley asked the audience. The audience cheered again.

She kept talking while she put the real tie in the right pocket. But just as she was about to pull the fake tie out of the left pocket—

"I'm sorry, Ashley," Mr. Barber said, grabbing the hat. "But I changed my mind. I can't let you do magic on my tie. It's too important to me."

"Mr. Barber," Ross said, putting an arm around his teacher. "Ashley is a trained professional. She'll get your tie back to you safe and sound."

Ross gently took the hat back from Mr. Barber. The teacher didn't say anything.

"Everything's fine, right, Ashley?" Ross said. He smiled at the audience.

"Right," Ashley said weakly. *The only problem*, she thought, *is that the hat's all turned around. How am I going to figure out which pocket is which?*

"All right," Ashley announced, whipping the scarf off. She pulled the tie from the left-hand pocket and lifted it out of the hat.

Quickly she took a huge pair of scissors and held them out to the audience. The audience cheered.

Ashley used the scissors to slowly cut the tie in half.

The audience screamed and cheered

again, but Mr. Barber looked totally freaked out.

"Don't worry," Ashley told him. "The energy field will keep your tie safe."

She lifted the silk scarf and once again showed the audience that the hat was empty. Then she dropped the two pieces of the cut tie back into the hat. She covered it again with the scarf, and put her hands inside.

Quickly she pulled the whole tie out of the right pocket and stuffed the cut pieces of necktie into the left one.

"Harrington, repairington," she said.

With a flourish she yanked off the scarf and pulled out the uncut tie.

"Tada!" Ashley announced, waving Mr. Barber's necktie for the crowd to see.

The crowd cheered again. I did it! Ashley thought. My trick was a big hit!

But Mr. Barber didn't look impressed. In fact, he stared at the back of his tie, his face furious.

"You'd better have an explanation for this," he said. "Because that is *not* my tie!"

To be continued … go to page 90

Mary-Kate and Ashley's
guide to school

When Mary-Kate and Ashley were filming, they had teachers around to make sure they didn't miss any lessons. Once they even used a cupboard as a classroom!

Try this quick quiz to find out if you're a Smartypants or a Partypants!

1

You have a heap of homework. You think:

a) Brill! I love maths anyway, and here's some more to do!
b) Oh well, at least it's an excuse for not doing the washing up tonight.
c) I am going to the cinema tonight. I'll do the homework in the morning – if I wake up in time!

2

How many school plays have you been involved with?

a) Every single one since infants – it means you get to spend even more time at school.
b) One or two – they're fun, but they're a big commitment.
c) Are you kidding? Spend valuable party time rehearsing?

3

Yay, it's the weekend! You plan to:

a) Spend the entire weekend in the library working on your project.
b) Get your homework done on Friday night so you can see your mates on Saturday.
c) Go out on Friday night, then spend the entire weekend shopping.

4

Someone slips you a note to pass on during class. You:

a) Keep the note and resolve to tear it up afterwards – no-one should interrupt lessons like that!
b) Pass it on if you can, but if you can't, too bad.
c) Open it and read it – if there's any gossip going, you need to know about it.

Dos and don'ts of school

Do keep a schoolwork diary so you always know when your homework and projects are due.

Don't leave your homework until the last minute.

Do arrive on time!

Don't stay up too late on a school night, however fab the TV is. You can always tape something and watch it later.

Do talk to your teacher if you're having problems – they're there to help you.

Don't forget that school is fun – it's where you get to goss with your mates, and learn loads of interesting stuff!

Mostly a's

Smartypants! You love school so much it's amazing you ever make it home in time for tea! Just remember there are other fun things to do – the last we heard, you couldn't buy clothes in school!

Mostly b's

You enjoy school, but you have lots of other interests as well. Sometimes you can be a bit of a rebel, but once in a while is OK... ssssort of!

Mostly c's

Partypants! You love having a good time, and feel school cramps your style. But remember the fun things, like break time, talking to your friends, school outings, discos and parties – it's not all bad, y'know!

Brain food

Make sure you have a filling, tasty and healthy lunchbox.

Try these:

tuna and cucumber wholemeal sandwiches

a pot of houmous and a pitta bread, carrot and celery sticks for dipping

granary roll filled with peanut butter and crunchy salad

Get organised

Want to be more organised for school? Try these tips.

★ Go through your room and get rid of all the stuff you don't need or use any more.

★ Set up a little study area. Your dressing table can double as a desk.

★ Keep your books and papers for each subject in a separate file or box.

★ Do your homework early. That way you can make more of your evening!

★ Check your uniform every night and make sure it's clean – no slinging it into the back of the wardrobe!

Anything can happen in a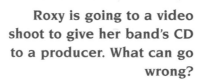

Mary-Kate and Ashley have been performing for the camera almost since they were born! Their latest movie is *New York Minute,* and the girls really had a blast filming. Follow their adventures and find out just how much can happen in a *New York Minute*!

Sisters Jane and Roxy Ryan have their New York day all planned. Jane is going to give an important speech that should get her a vital university scholarship.

Roxy is going to a video shoot to give her band's CD to a producer. What can go wrong?

Plenty! After getting into trouble on the train, the girls take a ride into town from a chauffeur in a fancy limo. But the chauffeur isn't all he seems...

When he chases the girls into a subway station, Roxy has to rely on some impressive kung fu moves to escape.

Then they get drenched by a passing car – can things possibly get any worse?

Can you imagine us running around New York City like this?

Jane & Roxy need a fashion change! In a nearby beauty parlour they undergo a major makeover…

Now all they have to do is make it to Jane's big speech at the university.

Think it all works out for Jane & Roxy?

Hey, anything can happen in a *New York Minute!*

Mary-Kate and Ashley's
word search and puzzles

Here are some more fun activities to keep you busy! There's a funky wordsearch and some fiendish puzzles for you to work out, so get cracking!

Here's another wordsearch for you to try. Hidden inside are a list of things you might find useful at school. See how many you can find. Remember, words can go forwards, backwards, up, down and diagonally.

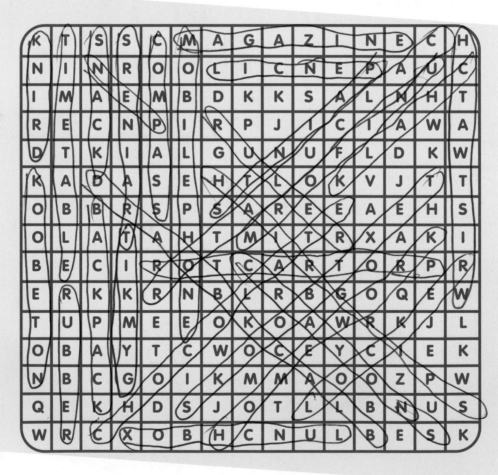

K	T	S	S	C	M	A	G	A	Z	I	N	E	C	H
N	I	N	R	O	O	L	I	C	N	E	P	A	U	C
I	M	A	E	M	B	D	K	K	S	A	L	N	H	T
R	E	C	N	P	I	R	P	J	I	C	I	A	W	A
D	T	K	I	A	L	G	U	N	U	F	L	D	K	W
K	A	D	A	S	E	H	T	L	O	K	V	J	T	T
O	B	B	R	S	P	S	A	R	E	E	A	E	H	S
O	L	A	T	A	H	T	M	I	T	R	X	A	K	I
B	E	C	I	R	O	T	C	A	R	T	O	R	P	R
E	R	K	K	R	N	B	L	R	B	G	O	Q	E	W
T	U	P	M	E	E	O	K	O	A	W	R	K	J	L
O	B	A	Y	T	C	W	O	C	E	Y	C	I	E	K
N	B	C	G	O	I	K	M	M	A	O	O	Z	P	W
Q	E	K	H	D	S	J	O	T	L	I	B	N	U	S
W	R	C	X	O	B	H	C	N	U	L	B	E	S	K

- BACKPACK
- BLACKBOARD
- CALCULATOR
- CHALK
- CHOCOLATE
- COMPASS
- CRAYONS
- DRINK
- GYM KIT
- HAIRGRIPS
- HOMEWORK
- LOCKER
- LUNCHBOX
- MAGAZINE
- MOBILE PHONE
- NOTEBOOK

- PAINTS
- PEN
- PENCIL
- PROTRACTOR
- RUBBER
- RULER
- SNACK
- TEXTBOOKS
- TIMETABLE
- TRAINERS
- UNIFORM
- WRISTWATCH

88

Letter search

Find the letter that ends the word on the left and begins the word on the right. Then unscramble them to reveal the name of a great Mary-Kate and Ashley movie!

DISC	O	LIVE
DUD	E	LATE
PA	W	HAT
HIND	I	RATE
BAT	H	ARE
MAT	E	BONY
TOR	N	EVER
PAL	M	ORE
TEE	N	EAR
TEA	R	ATE

When In Rome

(Answer: O, E, W, I, H, E, N, M, N, R = When in Rome)

Letter scramble

Unscramble these letters to find the names of five more Mary-Kate and Ashley videos!

HET LALHCGENE	The Challenge
SPTORPAS OT SARIP	PASSPORT TO PARIS
GTIGNITE ERETH	GETTING THERE
LOLRABIDB ADD	BILLBOARD DAD
URO SLIP EAR LADESE	OUR LIPS ARE SEALED
GINNIWN NDOOLN	WINNING LONDON

Answers: The Challenge, Passport to Paris, Getting There, Billboard Dad, Our Lips Are Sealed, Winning London)

 89

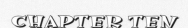

CHAPTER TEN

The audience fell silent. "Wh-what do you mean?" Ashley stammered.

"This tie is a fake," Mr. Barber declared, taking the tie from Ashley. "The tie I wear to school every day was autographed on the back by Mick Jagger!" Mary-Kate watched her sister's magic act from the wings. Her stomach tensed up and did a flip-flop.

Oh, no, Mary-Kate thought. *This is horrible!*

"Mick Jagger's autograph?" Ashley asked. "As in Mick Jagger, the lead singer of the Rolling Stones?"

Mr. Barber nodded. "I sat next to him on an airplane once, thirty years ago. He signed the back of my tie. That's why I wear it all the time."

Oh, no! Mary-Kate thought. *Ashley's trick is ruined!*

"I'm so sorry," Ashley said. She reached into the hat and pulled out the two pieces of Mr. Barber's original tie. "I meant to cut the other one, but you grabbed the hat and . . . and the ties must have got mixed up."

Mr. Barber took the pieces back from Ashley. He turned them over and stared at the back.

Ashley's in big trouble now, Mary-Kate thought. *Mr. Barber is going to lose it!*

But to her surprise, Mr. Barber didn't lose it. Instead, he gave a little shrug and sighed.

"At least the autograph isn't cut," Mr. Barber said. "And I guess it's all for the best."

"The best?" Ashley asked, surprised.

"Yup," Mr. Barber said. "I guess thirty years is a long time. I was getting tired of wearing the same tie every day."

Ashley's eyes popped wide open.

"It's time to kiss the past good-bye!" Mr. Barber announced.

The audience went wild. Mary-Kate could see Ashley sigh with relief. But Mary-Kate's heart was still pounding in her chest. Her sister might be out of the woods, but *she* was in deep trouble. Sugar still wasn't there.

Elliot marched over to her. "Okay, where is he?" he demanded. "We can't go on stage without a horse!"

"I don't know," Mary-Kate said. "J.D. should have been here by now."

Ashley and Ross ran past them off the stage.

"All right!" Mary-Kate heard Jeremy announce on stage. "And now it's time for the grand finale. Let's hear it for Elliot Weber and Mary-Kate Burke!"

"Come on," Elliot said. He jerked his head. "We'll have to do the trick ourselves!"

But an instant later, the big back door opened. J.D. was standing there with Sugar in tow.

"Wow! Just in time!" Mary-Kate cried.

She grabbed the reins from J.D. and Elliot walked on to the stage. He took a bow.

"Thank you, thank you," Elliot said. "And now, ladies and gentlemen, we have an incredibly special treat for you. My partner and I are going to demonstrate that even a horse can do card tricks. Ready, Mary-Kate?"

That was Mary-Kate's cue to walk Sugar on to the stage. She pulled on the horse's reins. But for some reason, the horse didn't move.

Mary-Kate got a sinking feeling in her stomach. She glanced down at the horse's ankle. Sure enough, there was the white patch.

Oh, no! Mary-Kate thought. *This is the wrong Sugar!*

CHAPTER ELEVEN

She hurried off stage and whispered to J.D., "Did you pick up this horse at Darcy's stables?"

J.D. looked confused. "No, why would I do that?" he asked.

Mary-Kate's heart pounded. She glanced back at the stage. Elliot was walking off stage towards them.

"What's going on?" he asked.

"This is the wrong horse," Mary-Kate wailed. "There was a mix-up." She explained what happened to Elliot and J.D.

"We can't go on stage now!" Elliot exclaimed. "We'll make fools of ourselves."

Mr. Thornbush, one of the Harrington teachers, walked by at that moment. "Don't be silly," he said. "You'll be great! You shouldn't have stage fright."

"But Mr. Thornbush, you don't understand—" Mary-Kate began.

"Now here we go. Onto the stage, the three of you." Mr. Thornbush took Sugar's reins and began to lead him onstage. Then he gave Mary-Kate and Elliot a little push in the same direction.

Mary-Kate glanced at Elliot. "It looks like we're doing this trick whether we want to or not," she whispered.

Elliot walked to the middle of the stage and slowly began his patter. "Sorry for the delay, folks," he announced. "But we're back, with Sugar . . . our wonder horse."

Mary-Kate wanted to melt into the floor.

"He's a really smart horse," Elliot went on. "I think you'll all be amazed to find out that Sugar can recognise all fifty-two cards in the deck!"

Elliot blindfolded himself so he couldn't see the cards. Then he spread out the deck of cards on the table, and told Mary-Kate to pick one.

Mary-Kate picked the six of diamonds and held it up for Sugar to see. Then she showed the card to the audience.

"What should I do now?" Mary-Kate asked Elliot.

"Put the card back in the deck any-

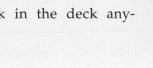

where you want," Elliot said.

Elliot went on with the act as he shuffled the cards. Then he finally pulled a three of clubs out of the deck.

He turned to face Sugar with the card in his right hand. "Is this your card?" Elliot asked the horse.

The horse just stood there.

Maybe I can help, Mary-Kate thought desperately. She nonchalantly strolled over to the horse and gave him a nudge.

The audience giggled.

"Maybe he's hard of hearing," Elliot joked. "Is this your card?" he said much louder.

Mary-Kate looked at Sugar and shook her head no. The audience laughed some more.

"Now, Sugar, I'm going to give you one more chance," Elliot said. He raised the card high and walked right up to Sugar's nose. "Is this the card Mary-Kate showed you?" he asked.

Sugar panicked. He started backing up, trying to get offstage. Mary-Kate grabbed his bridle but he kept moving.

The audience broke out in whispers. *This is hopeless*, Mary-Kate thought.

"Mary-Kate!" Ashley called from offstage. "Look!" She pointed to the door.

Mary-Kate glanced at the door. Then she gasped. Sean and Darcy were standing there. And with them was Darcy's horse!

Mary-Kate sighed with relief. That's the Sugar I've been looking for.

"Uh, ladies and gentlemen," Mary-Kate said, smiling. "As you can see, this horse isn't as smart as we thought he was. But in just a moment I plan to amaze you by transforming this dumb horse into a totally brilliant one!"

Everyone in the audience stopped whispering. Elliot opened his mouth to protest, but Mary-Kate quickly put her finger to her lips to shush him.

"All I need the audience to do is count to ten," she said.

The audience started counting. Mary-Kate signalled the stagehand to bring the curtain down.

"One! Two! Three! Four! Five!" she heard the audience say.

Mary-Kate waved to Sean to come and get the stubborn Sugar off the stage.

"What happened?" she asked him quickly.

"I realised I never told J.D. to go to Darcy's stables," Sean said quickly. "Big mistake. So here I am."

"Thank goodness!" Mary-Kate said.

She hurried to take the reins of Darcy's horse and bring the good Sugar on stage. Then she signalled to bring the curtain back up.

"Ladies and gentlemen, I think you will be amazed to experience the new brainpower of this horse," Mary-Kate said. "And now the great Elliot Weber will continue with his card trick."

"Um, right," Elliot said, pulling himself together. "Does everyone remember what the original card was?"

"Yes!" the audience shouted.

Elliot proceeded with the trick. First he held up his right hand and showed Sugar the three of clubs. "Is this your card?"

Sugar shook his head no, and the audience cheered.

Elliot showed him a ten of spades next. "Is this your card?" he asked Sugar.

Sugar shook his head no again. The audience clapped louder.

They love it! Mary-Kate thought happily.

"Is this your card?" Elliot asked, holding up a queen of hearts.

Sugar shook his head no. Mary-Kate could feel the audience sit up in their seats.

Elliot turned to the audience. "Ah!" he said. "I think I know what the problem is."

He walked over to the front of the stage and bent down. "Excuse me," he said to a woman sitting in the first row. "There's an envelope taped to the bottom of your chair. Could you hand it to me?"

The woman looked under her seat and gave him the envelope.

"Thank you," Elliot said.

He opened the envelope and took out a card. He showed it to Sugar. "Is this your card?" Elliot asked. He held it up with his left hand.

Sugar nodded his head up and down – and immediately Elliot spun round to show the card to the audience.

It was the six of diamonds. The right card!

The crowd went wild. Darcy jumped up and down in the wings, shouting, "That's my horse! That's my horse!"

"We did it!" Mary-Kate cheered, beaming with pride. She was so excited she gave Sugar *and* Elliot a hug!

"Su-gar! Su-gar!" Mary-Kate heard the audience cheer.

A moment later, Jeremy leaped back onto the stage.

"Let's give it up for all our magicians tonight!" he said, motioning for everyone to come on stage and take a bow.

But the audience did more than applaud. They jumped to their feet and gave the whole show a standing ovation.

Wow! Mary-Kate thought. *We're a hit*!

Ashley ran over and put an arm around her sister. "You did it!" she cheered. "You were fabulous!"

"So were you!" Mary-Kate said.

Elliot nudged Mary-Kate. "Our trick was the best! I'll be your partner anytime, Mary-Kate."

"Thanks, Elliot," Mary-Kate said. "But it almost didn't work out. I can't believe I made it through that trick and survived!"

"Hey – I survived being cut in half!" Ashley joked. "And I survived my first fight with Ross."

Mary-Kate smiled at her sister. "Isn't it great when everything works out in the end?"

"Yeah," Ashley answered. "It's just like magic!"

The End

mary-kateand